FLORIDA STATE
UNIVERSITY LIBRARIES

FEB 1 2001

TALLAHASSEE, FLORIDA

Ten Remarkable Women of the Tudor Courts and Their Influence in Founding the New World, 1530-1630

Front Cover: Mary Queen of Scots. Unknown artist.
By Courtesy of National Portrait Gallery, London.

TEN REMARKABLE WOMEN OF THE TUDOR COURTS AND THEIR INFLUENCE IN FOUNDING THE NEW WORLD, 1530-1630

Elizabeth Darracott Wheeler

Mellen Lives
Volume 11

The Edwin Mellen Press
Lewiston•Queenston•Lampeter

DA
317.3
.W47
2000

Library of Congress Cataloging-in-Publication Data

Wheeler, Elizabeth Darracott.
　Ten remarkable women of the Tudor courts and their influence in founding the New World, 1530-1630 / Elizabeth Darracott Wheeler.
　　p. cm. -- (Mellen lives ; v. 11)
　Includes bibliographical references (p.) and index.
　Contents: Queen Jane Grey -- Dorothée Stafford -- Queen Jeannne d'Albret -- Mary Queen of Scots -- Mary Dudley Sidney -- Mademoiselle Horsey – Margaret, Countess of Cumberland -- Mart St. Leger Grenville -- Bess Throckmorton Raleigh -- Eleanor White Dare.
　ISBN 0-7734-7717-9
　　1. Great Britain--History--Tudors, 1485-1603--Biography. 2. Great Britain--History--Early Stuarts, 1603-1649--Biography. 3. Great Britain--Colonies--America--History--16th century. 4. Great Britain--Colonies--American--History--17th century. 5. Great Britain--Court and courtiers--Biography. 6. America--Discovery and exploration--English. 7. Women--Great Britain--Biography. I. Mellen lives (Lewiston, N.Y.) ; v. 11.

DA317.3 .W47 2000
941.05'092'2--dc21
[B]
　　　　　　　　　　　　　　　　　　　　　　　　　　　　00-040192

This is volume 11 in the continuing series
Mellen Lives
Volume 11　ISBN 0-7734-7717-9
ML Series ISBN 0-88946-216-X

A CIP catalog record for this book is available from the British Library.

Copyright © 2000　Elizabeth Darracott Wheeler

All rights reserved. For information contact

　　　　The Edwin Mellen Press　　　　　　　The Edwin Mellen Press
　　　　　　　Box 450　　　　　　　　　　　　　　　Box 67
　　　　Lewiston, New York　　　　　　　　　Queenston, Ontario
　　　　USA 14092-0450　　　　　　　　　　CANADA L0S 1L0

The Edwin Mellen Press, Ltd.
Lampeter, Ceredigion, Wales
UNITED KINGDOM SA48 8LT

TABLE OF CONTENTS

	Acknowledgements	i
	Preface	iii
Chapter 1	Queen Jane Grey	1
Chapter 2	Dorothée Stafford	13
Chapter 3	Queen Jeanne d'Albret	25
Chapter 4	Mary Queen of Scots	39
Chapter 5	Mary Dudley Sidney	57
Chapter 6	Mademoiselle Horsey	69
Chapter 7	Margaret, Countess of Cumberland	83
Chapter 8	Mary St. Leger Grenville	97
Chapter 9	Bess Throckmorton Raleigh	111
Chapter 10	Eleanor White Dare	125
	Epilogue	139
	Endnotes	141
	Manuscripts, Calendars, Lists and Letters	161
	Bibliography	167
	Index	173

Acknowledgements

Manuscript sources ranged geographically from the University of Montreal to the British Museum, from the British Public Record Office to the French National Archives. Then the trail for artifacts led back to America and extended from the Chesapeake Bay to Boston, to the Caribbean and South America. Field trips included the Chateaux Country, Normandy, Russia, and the Mediterranean.

This search for history was stimulated by Professor Maude H. Woodfin of the University of Richmond, and by travels to libraries with my husband, Dr. Charles H. Wheeler III. Dr. Edwin Darracott Vaughan escorted us on a historical and fascinating tour along the south bank of the Pamunkey River to the fall line at Montevidio, and the South Anna River area in Virginia.

Browsing among stacks at the Alderman Library, University of Virginia, provided information about Jeanne d'Albret of Navarre, about privateering efforts of the English and French, and about their settlements. Primary materials available at the Virginia State Library substituted for the records of Hanover and New Kent County destroyed during the Revolutionary War and the Civil War. Choice rare books were found in the New York Public Library; and ship lists were consulted at the Swem Library, College of William and Mary. I appreciate the skillful assistance of Anne Wheeler Stratton. I am also grateful to Sara Darracott Wheeler, Charles Winston Wheeler, William D. Wheeler, Marcy S. Wheeler, Nancy P. Wheeler, Laura K. Wheeler, Howard W. Dobbins, and Mrs. Loveta I. Goodman. Susan Grayson, Dr. John R. Rilling, and Dr. Edward C. Peple and his wife Mary, gave impetus to the project.

In the Exeter Library, Devonshire, England, court records were made available to the author and her husband for this project. These included muniments of Exeter Cathedral. We stood at the baptismal font in St. Mary's Church, Bideford, Devon, where Lady Grenville's protegee, the American Indian "Rawly" was baptized. From Plymouth Hoe green we observed Sutton Pool where ships sailed westward towards America; and we visited Buckland Abbey, home of Sir Richard Grenville and of Sir Francis Drake. Recorded on the Mayor's chain were the names of ships that sailed with Drake to confront the Spanish Armada in 1577; these were supplied by Mr. G. A. Morris of Barnstaple Aethenaeum.

May the reader of *Ten Remarkable Women* experience the feelings of struggle and of romance belonging to the women contributors to the founding of America.

Elizabeth D. Wheeler

Preface

Vignettes of vivid feminine personalities in the Great Plan to Conquer the World reveal their influence. Partisans of Queen Jane Grey and their descendants led the way to the colonization of America. In some cases, women's dowries were essential for husbands to participate in the business of merchant adventuring. Wives and mistresses were involved, early death expected, and murder accepted among those with an indomitable spirit for founding colonies in America.

Each character in the founding of the new world was prominent at court during the reigns of Henry VIII, Edward VI, Mary Tudor, Queen Elizabeth I, or James I of England. As Jane Grey, nine-day-queen of England suggested, courageous women became involved with Protestant projects. Dorothée Stafford led young people in Switzerland, as did Jeanne d'Albret in France. Mary Dudley Sidney sacrificed her personal comfort for Queen Elizabeth. Mary Queen of Scots, tackled political problems. Mademoiselle Horsey harbored sea rovers, and her ideas stirred England.

The courage of these women was largely responsible for the interplay of trade between the colonists and the Mother Country. Mary St. Leger Grenville was recognized for bravery in Ireland. The stamina of Bess Throckmorton Raleigh was an inspiration. Margaret Russell Clifford, known as "Protestant Countess of the Royal Navy," helped shape the New World. And, Eleanor White Dare became the First Lady of Virginia, during the peopling and shaping of America.

Dr. John R. Rilling

Chapter 1
QUEEN JANE GREY
(1537 - February 12, 1554)

When Lady Jane Grey, nine-day-queen of England, was accused of high treason, her face reflected the Holy Spirit. Her sixteen years were affected by a plot to change the natural succession of the throne. The instigator of these plans, the duke of Northumberland, was interested in naval, military and civil affairs. When Jane witnessed the execution of her husband, Guildford Dudley, from her royal apartment in the Tower of London, she preparted a speech for her own death. Her courageous spirit during the dreadful plight of her life lived on in her poem.

> "Farewel, sweet Guildford! know, our end is near
> Heav's is our home, we are but strangers here:
> Let us make haste to go unto the blest,
> Which from these weary worldly labours rest.
> And with these lines, my dearest lord, I greet thee,
> Until in Heav'n thy Jane again shall meet thee."[1]

A genealogical chart in the family showed the young queen, born in 1537, was the eldest daughter of Sir Henry Grey, Marquis of Dorset and the Duchess of Suffolk, Frances Brandon. The latter was daughter of Charles Brandon by Mary Tudor, dowager of France, who was the daughter of Henry VII and sister to Henry VIII.[2]

Young Jane dressed gorgeously when Mary of Guise, Queen Regent of Scotland visited Richmond Palace on the Thames, and showed a special interest in Jane's portrait painted by an unknown artist.[3] Jane Grey, a teenager, and possible successor to the English throne, knew Greek, Latin, Hebrew, French and Italian. She wrote, "One of the greatest benefits that God gave me is that He sent me so sharp and severe parents and so gentle a schoolmaster, for when I am in the presence of either father or mother, whether I speak, keep silence, sit, stand, go, eat, drink, be merry, or sad. . .I must do it. . .even so perfectly as God made the world. . .or else I am so sharply taunted, so cruelly threatened, yea presented sometimes with pinches, nips and bobs and other things. . .I think myself in Hell till the time comes when I must go to Mr. Aylmer who teacheth me so gently, so pleasantly and with such pure allurements to learn."[4]

Schooled in the requirements for royalty, while being trained by her parents to be queen of England, Jane's face reflected a quiet inner joy because she studied the Protestant religion. In their home in old Bradgate Castle in Leicestershire, surrounded by terraces and extensive walls, she memorized the Ten Commandments, repeated the Lord's Prayer regularly, and piously sang Protestant hymns. However, the Catholic church meanings of extreme unction, and last rites of a person's life, and purgatory, were unexplained to her. Superstitions and the ways a person died in grace were meaningless. The priest of the Old Learning did not hear her confession of sins. The child Jane talked to God in silence, in the New Learning.

The princess practiced high standards of living in the strict environment of Bradgate castle. Her breakfast diet included meat, ale, and various servings of wheat, corn, and nut bread. Her appropriate daily activities included the study of languages and reading French aloud. Playing the pianoforte and strumming the harp were part of her routine.

Whether exercising, playing the harp, or dancing, Jane dressed befittingly for each event. Because her mother, Frances Brandon, was addicted to sports and promoted hawking expeditions, her daughter's hunting outfits were similar to those of jockeys. To appease her mother, Jane followed fox hounds on hunts into miles of thickly wooded park land beyond the old Bradgate terraces. However, when animals were killed, and birds beheaded and defeathered, the young girl concluded hunting was a cruel sport. Filled with resentment about killing rabbits and hawking parties, she reluctantly obeyed maternal commands about clothes.

Quietly parting from the hunters, Jane communed with nature and with

Chapter1: Queen Jane Grey

God. Walking along streams and slopes of slate quarries, she meditated among ferns bordering the lake. She practiced a religious schedule for making her body a Temple of God. Like those of the Protestant Learning of John Calvin, Jane behaved better out of church and worshipped better inside the sanctuary.[5]

Her mother rarely praised this daughter, and her father was unpredictable. Properly attired in a damask skirt of green satin trimmed with velvet, the teenager conversed in French with family guests. When trumpets were sounded in the Great Hall gallery, and each course of the feast was announced after the music, Jane's face lost animation. At her mother's command to practice waltz steps in an adjacent parlor with her humpback sister, Katherine, Jane obeyed in a half-hearted fashion. She rebelled against parental instructions.[6]

Sir Henry Grey's eldest daughter, extremely atune to the New Learning, expressed her anger about his lack of interest in religion and his pride in royal endeavors. She memorized Latin declensions and foreign languages. Greek phrases appeared in her letters written in Latin to his New Learning group in the Alps. Her letters to German Calvinists in exile in mountains near Zurich, Switzerland, were promptly answered by her father's friends. To them, Jane became known for her wisdom.[7]

While Sir Henry Grey was occupied in Strasburg with merchants, Jane listened to the positive statements of his favorite guests in the parlour at Bradgate castle. They told the child the latest startling news that lingered in her mind: Henry VIII welcomed French Protestants in England, and allowed them to purchase land. From the charming guest Martin Bucer, Jane learned his idea was that anyone who shrank from labor had no rights to food and support. At Bucer's funeral, princess Jane, among the three thousand mourners, wept openly for her friend, her favorite guest at Bradgate.[8]

The custom of children of royal families of various countries was to visit in royal households for months at a time. Therefore, eleven-year-old princess Jane visited the Queen Dowager, Katherine Parr, the sixth wife of Henry VIII. The young girl realized the king's legs wobbled as a result of gout and aided the friendly, apprehensive queen with occasional massages for the king. She walked with the queen's group to admire the greyhounds, flowers, and parrots. After the kind school master, Robert Asham, taught Jane and young Edward VI to assume a gentle tone of voice, the queen's study groups at Chelsea praised her ability to read in an appropriate tone from Katherine Parr's *Prayers and Meditations*.[9]

The reason why the charismatic Puritan preacher Dr. Hooper, Bishop of Gloucester, refused to wear ecclesiastical vestments was because he considered them unchristian inventions. At powerful sermons, he offered ideas similar to those of John Calvin and Protestants about the New Learning. And, Jane was impressed.[10] This seven-year-old child had been informed on 12 July 1543 about a marriage proposal, in the royal apartment at Whitehall Palace next to those of the king. The plan, part of a political plot, was for Jane to become the bride of the frail boy king Edward VI, son of Henry VIII by Jane Seymour. She had enjoyed court associations with the lad Edward, until the rumor of their possible marriage circulated. As years passed, she studied the English law, "Marriage equals the communion of man and woman. . .certain words hinder a contract of marriage, such as the bridegroom being mad, deaf, dumb."[11] Jane interpreted this law to mean she should not marry the boy king because Edward was suffering from a strange illness. And, her opinion about this union was confirmed in first complete English Bible by Miles Coverdale.

Jane discovered a long alliance with royalty resulted in loss of happiness and privacy. While traveling at a fast pace with the royal household from palace to palace for feasting and masques, her way of life at home became near and dear to her. While enduring late nights of gaiety on various journeys, she fell ill with a fever, and doctors ordered several weeks of rest cure. Shortly after attending the funeral of her dear friend, Queen Katherine Parr, Jane returned to life with her family.[12]

Strange circumstances encircled an existence at court, and there were constant struggles among the visitors. By the time she was fifteen, Jane encountered scheme after scheme of John Dudley, Admiral of England, known as the duke of Northumberland who served as Vicount L'Isle on King Edward's privy council. She was an important royal tool to Northumberland, grandmaster of the realm, who was active in naval, military, and civil affairs. His chief aim was to find gold for England. For English ships to claim territory for England, and to discover trade to Russia, he proposed 4,000 soldiers sail to explore Cathay via the Northwest. Another typical plan of the admiral was to send ships by the Northeast to Cathay to hunt for gold. Unwillingly, Jane became a political tool in the hands of this powerful politician.[13]

Northumberland's cunning scheme concerning the successor to the throne of England included Jane Grey and John Dudley's son. His stern proposal was to perform three marriages in one extravagant wedding ceremony conducted with Protestant rites. In these nuptials his son Guildford Dudley and Jane Grey were to become husband and wife. His daughter Katherine was to marry Lord Hastings, and her younger sister would be the bride of Lord Herbert. Jane had the helpless feeling of a political pawn when these marriage plans were adopted by her father and Northumberland. For her, this was a distasteful plot.[14]

Another part of the scheme concerned an investigation of Jane's lineage and the wish of Henry VIII. According to the king's will, after the boy king Edward VI died, Mary, daughter of Catherine of Aragon, and Elizabeth, daughter of Anne Boleyn, were eligible to wear the crown of England. Following these successors to the crown came the Suffolk line, and then the Stuarts. During the discussions of the inheritance of her parents and grandparents, Jane prayed for a pure outcome.

The boy, King Edward VI, suffering from a strange illness, was counseled in private about an alternate plan for succession to the throne of England. This excluded his half-sisters Mary and Elizabeth on grounds of illegitimacy. The crown of England and Protestant values of the Reformation would pass to up-coming queen Jane Grey, of the Suffolk line, at the death of King Edward VI. This seemed agreeable to the youth.

This Protestant plan was also sponsored by hot gospeller Edward Underhill, and vice-chancellor of Cambridge Sir Edwin Sandys. Another proponent was Jane's relative, Sir Francis Russell. At the house of Sir William Cecil, councilors attending conferences on the sacrament spoke openly for the cause of the crown. The king's religious instructor, Dr. Richard Cox, wanted a Protestant monarch, and merchants sanctioned this proclamation.[15] The declaration that Lady Jane Grey was to be the successor to the crown of England was due to Northumberland. He had persuaded members of the King's Council and the judges to verify this statement when Letters Patent about the plan were signed by King Edward VI. Furthermore, the the will of King Edward included these judges' signatures on 21 June 1553, after the boy king guaranteed his approval.

While Edward VI was king, Jane approved the monarchy. However, the marriage intricacies of this complicated plot were frightening. Other shrewd moves concerning the succession to the throne of England involved Jane's mother, Frances Brandon, and her father, Sir Henry Grey. Her parents were persuaded to relinquish their claims to the throne. And, Jane had no opportunity to choose her own husband.[16] Jane suffered from shock from the idea of linking the house of Suffolk to Northumberland. The thought of becoming the successor queen of England and wife of fifteen-year-old Guildford, the fourth son of Northumberland and Anne (Guildford), caused the princess to tremble with fright. From her heart, she stated the crown was a great temptation to be resisted. And she insisted one of Edward's sisters assume this responsibility. She realized Northumberland and his political friends plotted to secure the succession to the English throne to his own family. The arrangements to conduct her wedding ceremony at the military center at Durham Palace located above the River Wear disgusted Jane. Her childish face reflected disapproval.

That fateful wedding took place at Durham Palace high on a hill overlooking the River Wear. After the bride slid reluctantly into her secretly designed wedding gown with diamonds and seed pearls on brocaded gold and silver material, a maid-of-honor plaited Jane's honey-colored hair with strings of pearls.[17]

Three sets of the vows of matrimony were exchanged between three sets of children at the colorful wedding, and her parents, council members, and the Dudley family were present. And, masques and jousts of royal splendor were among the extravagant festivities in the Strand. After the sumptuous feast, several aldermen experienced food poisoning.[18]

Chapter1: Queen Jane Grey

Jane's poem revealed,

> "At Durham palace, where sweet Hymen sang,
> Whose buildings with our nuptial music rang:
> Where great Dudley match's with noble Grey,
> When they devis'd to link, by wedlock's band,
> The house of Suffolk to Northumberland.[19]

Exhausted from lack of endurance, the bride returned home with her sister and parents. She happily resumed studying, and breathed a sigh of relief because the wedding day arrangements failed to include the consummation of a loveless marriage.[20]

In spite of her conscience and qualms, Jane was declared Queen of England in a ceremony at Greenwich Palace on the Thames. The lord mayor of London, aldermen, merchants of the staple, and merchant adventurers, jointly responsible for the decision on 9 July 1553, were present.[21]

When the young queen and attendants prepared to leave Greenwich Palace for London, numerous bystanders expressed their opinions about the barge transporting the group of royalty. Some thought Mary, daughter of Catherine of Aragon, should succeed to the crown of England, and others desired that Mary, Queen of Scots, should hold the scepter. On 10 July 1553, Protestant Queen Jane, her mother, her maid-of-honor Anne Throckmorton, and sister-in-law Mary Dudley Sidney, sailed on the Thames from Greenwich Palace to the Tower of London.

When trumpets startled bystanders, followed by the announcement that Lady Jane Grey was the new monarch of England, not a cap was thrown in the air, nor was a scarf waved in welcome. As the barge approached the Tower of London, to English gathered on the banks of the Thames, it was obvious this queen was not the choice of the majority of the crowd. A silence of fright prevailed.[22]

The public acknowledgement aggravated Jane's composure. Clutching the stomacher blazing with diamonds, she was extremely self-conscious about gems on her gown of gold cloth. Attempting to hide the priceless drop pearl and the necklace set with rubies, she hastily pulled a purple velvet surcoat bordered with ermine close to her body.

Guildford, dressed in a white satin suit trimmed with gold and a collar of diamonds, heard his wife whisper she preferred a simple life to that at Greenwich Palace or in the Tower of London. Jane felt she was usurping the throne in a lawless way, and she acquiesced reluctantly. To gracefully accept the scepter to rule the English nation, this Queen summoned all the dignity could muster.

Sorrowfully, the Queen stated, "My liberty is better than the chain you offer me!"[23]

Her Majesty, smiling wanly beneath the canopy of gold, with shaking hands held the crown, heavy with jewels. Late in the day, the queen, shuttering from insecurity, was pompously presented the keys to the Royal Apartments in the Tower of London by her father-in-law, Northumberland.[24] While the sun set on the royal barge, ladies-in-waiting followed an unsteady bride planning to join Guildford later at his family home.

Entering the Tower for safety, the Queen firmly announced, "The succession to the throne is mine, and I order that I be secured in possession of it."[25]

Jane observed the Tower of London, constructed of stone resting on stone, was surrounded by a mound with blood stains. And, the Queen's House where Anne Boleyn had spent her last days served the dual purpose of a royal residence and a state prison. The castle carpenters appeared with axes dangling from their necks, and planes hanging at their sides. Jane saw timber, with holes bored and the surface smoothed, dragged from ships to a spot for military use.[26]

Each jewel brought from the vault beneath the Tower of London, and slowly tried on by the sixteen-year-old queen, caused her to hate her appearance. She abhorred living on this station where it would fall her duty to control the military. Indeed, her weakness to deal with the soldiers importing armies from France made this impossible.

Because the war-mongering lords supported Mary, half-sister of Edward VI, Queen Jane was severly annoyed. When she made Guildford a duke, foreign ambassadors upset her by calling Guildford "king." And, when her husband used witty persuasions to bring help and munitions from France, he disturbed the peace. And, those soldiers prepared for war pursued the noisy army of Northumberland.[27]

On 19 July 1553 the "nine-day-queen of England" received the fateful news

Chapter 1: Queen Jane Grey

that the Council had declared Mary, daughter of Catherine of Aragon, queen. Jane's joyful smile showed she really wanted Mary to be queen. With tears streaming, and her mind full of staggering thoughts, she persuaded her father to forsake her defenders, and to stay with her in the Tower. The startling news about Sir Henry Grey becoming a prisoner indicated enemies were plotting the destruction of Jane, ex-queen of England. When her father-in-law, the duke of Northumberland, was arrested, Sir Francis Russell was on the high seas, and Jane was helpless in the Tower.[28]

Jane and Guildford, prisoners in their solitary confinement, heard guards stomp and bolt doors at night. At sunrise, soldiers removed the canopy of state from her entrance. People wondered whether the ex-queen and her maid-of-honor would be accused of high treason.

She wrote to Guildford:

> "They which begot us did beget this sin,
> They first begun what did our grief begin,
> We tasted not, 'twas they which did rebel
> (Not our offence) but in their fall we fell."[29]

From the window of her room in the Tower, Jane heard the lusty crowd shouting, as they climbed Tower Hill to witness the beheading of the duke of Northumberland.[30] Her terror was well-founded when she dropped on her knees, begging for God's guidance. She prayed for Him to defend her with his spirit until the end. And, she yearned for eternal life.

Several months passed. Clasping a book in her hand, Jane bravely followed the ax-carrier and archbishop on foot from the Tower. The black velvet volume hanging before her matched the gown and edging of her French hood. Weeping gentlewomen slowly followed with faltering steps to the Guild Hall, where Jane and Guildford calmly pleaded guilty, and returned to solitary confinement.[31]

Guildford, alone in his Tower apartment, and granted a reprieve, rashly helped organize another insurrection with the group of soldiers marching to Deptford. They crossed the river in Admiral Winter's boats, and charged Brass Mount. Guildford was arrested again.[32]

During her imprisonment, the pious ex-queen listened to the sound of scaffolding being erected on Tower Green. The priests sent by Queen Mary attempted to persuade Jane to forsake the Protestant religion for Catholicism. Realizing death was imminent, Jane bravely withdrew to her bedchamber to meditate and pray. Her letter to her irresponsible father expressed sympathy about his woeful imprisonment and his death sentence. She indicated he hastened her death by joining rioters, but she consoled him by saying they would meet in heaven.[33] Writing in Greek, Jane begged her sister Katherine to learn to die, to be steadfast, and to put on the breast plate of righteousness. The "nine-day-queen" urged her maid-of-honor to encourage her unborn child to become involved with a Protestant project. A double execution of the innocent couple on the scaffold would certainly affect a crowd.[34]

Contemplating death, instead of proposing a last interview with Guildford, Jane reread her poem of comfort, "Farewel, sweet Guildford; know, our end is near..."

She felt sorrow would overwhelm them and destroy the firmness needed for composure. Preparing Guildford to be separated from her but a moment, she suggested they would rejoin each other and be together forever. Heaven would be their home. The ex-queen of England urged her maid-of-honor to smile and to encourage her unborn child to become involved with a Protestant project.

The Tower guard whispered to Jane of Guildford's love and affection, and pointed to his indelible inscriptions "Iane" [Jane] on his window and wall in the Tower.[35]

From her window, Jane watched Guildford follow the executioner across the courtyard, and saw him look upward for a glimpse of his wife. He stepped upon the scaffold on Tower Hill, and strained in vain to see her face--until his head rolled on the block. Jane uttered a cry of anguish as his headless corpse on straw in a cart passed her window. Briefly, Jane relived the splendor of their wedding ceremony. She had watched the beheading.

On 12 February 1554 onlookers saw the "nine-day queen" of England mount a private scaffold on Tower Green with dignity, and the maid-of-honor open the Protestant Prayer Book. Although she felt nausea arising, Jane calmly delivered her

Chapter1: Queen Jane Grey

memorized speech to the people. She admitted her crime against Queen Mary, and she remembered childhood days in court. Jane appealed to her sympathizers, "Please witness I am a true Christian."[36] Handing her robe to her maid-of-honor with serenity, Jane's face reflected the light of the Holy Spirit. She placed her head on the wooden block, awaiting the ax of the executioner, and prayed she and Guildford would lie side by side in St. Peter's Chapel.

Jane left her poetry and writings intact. With this in hand, her sister Katherine composed the chart with family genealogy. Some readers felt the sins of the two fathers was pride, and this caused the overthrow of their children. Open adherents of the claim of Lady Jane Grey to the throne included Sir Edwin Sandys, Edward Underhill, and John Calvin. They spoke out for her cause.

Courageous Jane Grey stimulated the flight of Protestants.

Chapter 2
DOROTHÉE STAFFORD, Seigneuress de Rocheford
(1532 -1604)

Dorothy Stafford, Seigneuress de Rocheford, and princess of the wardrobe of Queen Elizabeth, legally inherited the crown jewels of Anne Boleyn. The second wife of Sir William Stafford realized these pearls, rubies, diamonds and emeralds had also belonged to Catherine of Aragon and changed owners several times. The disposal of these prized possessions depended upon the owner's generosity and interest in the New Learning programs.[1]

Widower Sir William Stafford's first wife Mary Boleyn, had inherited the jewels of her sister Anne, daughter of the French ambassador Thomas Boleyn. The marriage of King Henry VIII to Anne Boleyn was consummated privately, officially, and under the proper authorities in England. However, when the Pope refused to sign a divorce decree of King Henry VIII from Catherine of Aragon, the Privy Council of England had taken specific action. These crown jewels were legally awarded to Anne Boleyn, and were kept locked in a trunk.

After Queen Anne Boleyn, charged with treason in 1536, appeared at a short trial in the Tower of London, she was beheaded. According to a written will, her crown jewels were bequeathed to her sister, Mary (Boleyn) Stafford. Following Mary's death, her husband married his cousin Dorothy. Then the pearls, diamonds, rubies, sapphires and emeralds of Catherine of Aragon became the exclusive property of his new wife wherever she resided. Anne Boleyn's execution, the turning point in English history, had changed the balance of power in 1536. When the Church of England was formed, the Catholics became unpopular. The birth of

Elizabeth, unwanted daughter of King Henry VIII and Anne, took place at Hampton Court Castle before the trial. And, the presence of Elizabeth was a real problem for authorities in England.

Four-year-old cousin Dorothy, daughter of Baron Stafford and his wife Ursula, was of a comparable age, when the princess was sent away from London to visit in Kent. Nearby was the fortified manor Allington Castle, and Hever Castle, and Leeds Castle where her mother and the king had resided. These cousins shared the sorrowful outcome of the queen's trial and pitied Anne Boleyn. These children became life-long friends.[2]

Dorothy wept with grief with the princess. News of the well-publicized trial, culminating in the dreadful beheading of the queen, the king's second wife, affected people in Kent. The cousins followed the path over extensive farmland to St. Peter's Chapel near Hever Castle. They admired the white sheep and goats in the meadows and left the carriage to pick grapes in the orchards. They were determined to follow the path to the cemetery nearby to pay tribute to Anne Boleyn, mother of Elizabeth. At the cemetery, Dorothée and the Princess discovered the body of the queen buried in a disgraceful fashion in a chest made of elm wood. At this dreadful site, shrieks filled the chapel, and tears streamed down the children's faces.[3]

Past the dairies near Leeds Castle the carriages paused at the battlemented gate house. The passengers learned the queen had enjoyed the luxury of romancing on these grounds until the bell and clock struck parting time. Inside this castle, surrounded by an atmosphere of fortune, they saw hand-crafted oak panelling, and the brasses rubbed by ambassador Thomas Boleyn in accordance with the French tastes. The refined teak furniture in the Gloriette Apartment, was queen Anne's choice to transform the stylish room that included charming windows and candles. Walnut chests in a casket with compartments in the royal rooms beyond the Banqueting Hall had held Anne's legally acquired crown jewels.[4]

Princess Elizabeth was thirteen when she waited for Dorothy under Astronomical Clock over the Queen Anne Gateway to Hampton Court Castle. Overhead were royal coat-of-arms and carved medallions of Roman emperors modeled in terra cotta. The girls observed the intricate mechanisms of the amazing

Chapter 2: Dorothée Stafford

clock ticking away the hour and day of the month. They counted the number of days since the beginning of the year, and observed the two phases of the moon and its "southing." Bystanders calculated the approximate time of high water at London Bridge. And, the teenagers monitored the weather vanes rotating on the castle turrets.[5]

Beyond the wrought iron gates was the Great Fountain Garden, and three avenues connecting a vast semi-circle of trees and water that stretched across Home Park. Dorothy and Princess Elizabeth participated in sumptuous parties for courtiers while Katherine Parr was queen. On the newly constructed tennis court of Hampton Court castle they enjoyed the new tennis game with English rules. This land was formerly leased by the Knights of St. John of Jerusalem when ties had existed between England and the Papacy. From the threshold of the king's Drawing Room, they admired the wreath holding the heads of cherubs at the marble chimney surrounded by handsome tapestries. They climbed to various floors and visited the bare boudoir of princess Mary, daughter of Catherine of Aragon, who was eligible for the crown.[6]

Dorothy's family devoted energy to Protestants when the political arena was greatly altered during the reign of the boy king Edward VI. Calvinism had come into the open. They understood the goodness associated with the New Learning Program.[7]

The alarming religious situation that reversed to Catholic during the reign of Queen Mary was squarely faced by the Stafford family. The trial for treason and execution on the scaffold of the "nine-day-queen" had ended in turmoil. Shortly afterwards, this queen's Protestant relatives met the same fate. Some of the nobility, like the Staffords, were hunted, and beheaded. Others were imprisoned and burned at stake between 1555 and 1558.[8]

Shortly after Dorothy married widower, cousin Sir William Stafford, the family fled from England. According to the note written from the Tower of London by prisoner Thomas Cramner, Archbishop of Canterbury, he was scheduled for execution. The contents of this message urged Protestants to flee for their lives. This affected the Stafford family.[9] Over eight hundred persons with anti-Catholic leanings appealed for help from the secret cabinet financed by Queen Jane Grey's uncle, Sir Francis Russell.[10] However, with assistance from a jailor, he fled from London to challenge the supremacy of Spain.[11]

The crown jewels of England, after the untimely death of Mary, had become the property of Sir William Stafford's wife Dorothy. She feared these would cause her to be hunted and persecuted, even beheaded. In private, aided by her husband, she wrapped each priceless item in the chest, and tied a purse containing precious jewels securely around her waist. The Stafford family and their servants sought transportation abroad. Their horse-drawn caravan was headed towards the English Channel with necessities of voluntary exiles.[12]

Dorothy, for security reasons, whispered to the mysterious French captain of their ship that her name recorded on the passenger list was written "Dorothée" with an accent. The admiral possessed good navigational skills, and displayed some knowledge of astronomy. Among these family exiles boarding the nameless ship were Sir William Stafford, known as Seigneur in France, and Dorothy his wife. Jane, his sister, and mistress Sandes, their cousin, followed. Then, Edward his son, Elizabeth his daughter, John Watson, Arthur James registered. Accompanying them were Edmunde, his servants, and Elizabeth his maiden. While traveling, Dorothée periodically searched her attire to determine the position of the royal jewels hidden in the purse on the belt around her waist. Her attitudes were of paramount importance for the safe arrival of the crown jewels.[13]

The Staffords, now English refugees, secretly sailed on the rough seas towards uncharted waters of the Bay of Biscay, probably to the Pau River where Anne Boleyn had sailed. In these seas, Admiral Coligny assured Protestant exiles freedom of worship, and libertines were kept from being destroyed by persecution. Many headed for St.-Jean-de-Luz, the chief port of the Pyrenees, where Queen of Navarre, Marguerite, had afforded asylum to Queen Anne Boleyn at Pau Castle, Navarre.[14]

Queen Marguerite helped ministers visiting in Pau Castle to found a French church in Strasburg. Among them were William Farrall, Master of the college of the Cardinal le Moine in Paris, and the Protestant theological student John Calvin.[15]

She was attracted by the grace and virtue revealed in Calvin's love of the truth, and she respected his stern morality and his grave inner life. She encouraged this student to persuade Catholics to help with the work of God.[16] Later, the Protestant religion was proclaimed in Pau.[17]

Dorothée's exiled family possibly fled incognito on large white horses from the seashore through the independent states of Navarre and Bearn and skirted the Pyrenees. Some groups on foot followed the course of the Pau River, and some climbed, then slid on glaciers down mountains. When these exiles reached the Rhone River, they boarded a small boat.

Dorothée planned to settle in Geneva, known as the City of God. The reputation of this independent republic, once renowned for pleasure and fairs, had changed. Protestants respected this city for piety that was far from corruption. New arrivals heard the great bell Clemence toll, summoning families to church. Exiles marveled at the blue waters from Lake Leman that ran into those of the Rhone. They remembered the fruitful vineyards below the glaciers on Mont Blanc, and Dorothy sought Calvin's newly established church.

Appearing as a plain person on Geneva streets, she wore a nondescript cape, with the hood of her bonnet hanging free. Her dress was lifted from the ground as a safeguard. English nobles from Strasburg had flocked into Geneva through a frequented Alpine pass. Merchants were in the City of God from Spain, Normandy, Flanders, Venice, and Tuscany. Catholic ministers threw away images and their vestments, as well as organs, bells and candles. The Protestants seeking plain meeting houses with Bibles instead of St. Pierre's ornate Catholic church included the Stafford family. They frequently heard Calvin assert Geneva was, "the most perfect school of Christ that ever was on earth since the days of the apostles."[18]

Dorothée conversed with French refugees and street-smart cloth merchants who had fled with merchandise on mules from Emden to Cologne, to Geneva. Poor wanderers had been welcomed to German hospitality in the busy mart in the courtyard of Frankfort on the Main. A man with committed beliefs towards God and salvation had left Frankfort, and trudged to Geneva where he knew John Calvin. Dorothée listened to discussions about how trouble began over the Latin liturgy that omitted Purgatory. Some controversies had arisen over the dogmas of the Lord's Supper and the lawfulness of infant baptism.[19]

Honest yeomen were erecting a plain Protestant church to be named Calvin's Church in Geneva. One congregation of statesmen worshiped in the ornate St. Pierre Church. In this city run by Calvinists, punishments were heavy for gambling and blasphemy. Spies were appointed to hunt prostitutes, and the punishment for adultery was death. To sing a lewd song was considered a crime, and dancing was prohibited. The power of the libertines was completely broken.

Dorothée heartily supported missions. From the secret purse on her belt, she exchanged precious rubies and sparkling diamonds to help the sick. In 1555, she contributed her crown jewels to purchase supplies for poor people in three ships under Admiral Coligny. These colonists hoped to to found a Geneva in the wilderness. Dorothee also contributed to a colony at Port Royal, Florida.[20] She assumed the title Seigneuress de Rocheford to indicate she was the wife of an English nobleman in exile.[21]

By 13 October 1555, Dorothée purchased a vacant old castle located on the snow-capped Alps where goats and sheep were abundant. This Alpine estate was suitable for housing refugees and students, and adequate accommodations existed for her family and fleeing nobles.

At home in this old Alpine castle, the Protestant seigneuress set an example for living a normal existence in exile. She considered conjugality and romance important in a fashionable way of life. Her example rubbed off on students who helped gardeners plant vegetables, and on peasants who toted these to the infirm and sick. When carpenters crafted furniture for new houses, fears were replaced by work. The names of exiles seeking security in Dorothée's castle read like a catalogue of nobility. Included were Margery Knox, wife of John Knox, and her mother Elizabeth, and the Bodleigh family. Kate Knollys's family also risked their lives for the Protestant cause.[22]

By the first of November 1555, Dorothée greeted Protestant ministers and listened to their ideas in the newly erected church. Children were taught to never use profane language, nor should they play cards or sing bawdy songs. Amusements on

Sunday were forbidden.[23]

Calvin emphasized, "Childhood is like an empty vase, conserving the odor of the first liquid poured into it."[24]

When refugees in her household suffered deep-seated anger and frustration, Dorothee suggested rest and relaxation. She encouraged each exile to fulfill a particular role in the Christian mission movement. She encouraged them to exercise by playing balloon ball or tennis, for a balanced life. Children whipped the top, while teenagers walked on stilts, and other athletes skated on ice. During the day, they sought the Grace of God on the mountain, and turned to the stars at night.

Dorothée relied on faith and her own wits. She planned elegant dinner parties at proper intervals. She used a theme to promote conversation about colonization among the English who had experienced the atrocities of relatives being burned or beheaded. Her long table was covered with an appliqued Swiss tablecloth and adorned with golden candlesticks stolen from a Spanish cathedral. The lace-edged napkins were embroidered by children in a nearby Spanish convent. Because some guests had witnessed their relatives being drawn and quartered, few felt guilty about using these appointments. Dorothée assumed the role of a servant of God who brought good news of God's love and forgiveness.

The seigneuress anticipated problems stemming from educational questions before the guests arrived. After reading the Psalms in prose with a close confidante, she planned conversations to help heal hates and prejudices. Her invitation to a sumptuous feast was issued to a minister who refused to concede in the controversy about ceremonials in the English liturgy. Although she disliked anabaptists and members of the Family of Love, she dealt kindly with Kate Knollys. Prone to be hostile and resentful of radical Protestant leanings, her calm countenance served as a catalyst for troubles.

Sometimes Dorothée was torn apart from her sister, Jane, because of the political opinions of professors. And, obviously the outspoken minister John Knox hated the English liturgy.[25] Also, a special messenger, a minister, brought news from wealthy widow Catherine Brandon who remarried merchant Richard Bertie after her husband's death. This minister had traveled incognito from Venice to

Padua to report that Catherine expected to give birth in exile to a possible candidate for the English throne.[26]

In the Alpine castle were talented young people, including bearded students who habitually sipped ale while discussing bizarre killings in their hometowns. After strawberries and custard, they composed propaganda pamphlets directed against Catholics. Under supervision they printed pamphlets and "seditious" literature for distribution in Protestant churches in Geneva and abroad.[27] To some impassioned conversations about education, the political opportunities to market educational goods in the New World, even a "paper war," was stressed by the hostess.

She encouraged the Calvinist student Walter Travers to attend the free schools to study Latin, English, and Hebrew, as well as some math. He discussed the scriptures in his winning way, without a license. She helped John Bodleigh and his wife receive the exclusive right to publish an English Bible with illustrations. She also encouraged artist Nicholas Hilliard.[28]

It was difficult to believe the teachings of the religious organizer John Knox although he was well-versed in Bible narratives. When Knox left Geneva and returned to Scotland, with a doctrine subversive of all authority, he was extremely vehement against the Catholic queen, Mary Stuart. He pressed the Lords of the Congregation in Scotland for reform. Morning and night, as in Geneva, those of the reformed religion were supposed to attend the preaching of the Gospel in the established Protestant church.[29]

On 12 August 1556, an envoy from the Coligny colony on the Amazon River returned to the church of St. Pierre. The ministerial student reported that although some savages in the American wilderness made public confessions of faith, it was impossible to establish a Protestant colony there.[30] Although this project was abandoned, the spirit of converting the natives thrived among the few returnees. Special recognition was given to the first settlers to cross the Atlantic Ocean.[31]

The teachings of Calvin changed Dorothée's way of life. She learned a disciple was committed only to God and his word. A person who satisfied the will

Chapter 2: Dorothée Stafford

of God would be saved through belief in Jesus Christ. People were predestined for heaven rather than hell because of moral behavior. Among the Protestant groups in Geneva, work and play were prohibited on Sunday. Students could not go to the theater, nor dance, play cards, curse, or drink. The church and state became harmonious. Leaders were called kings because theoretically they had been elected by God, while the monarchs of the earth were despised.

Faith was Dorothée's highest virtue. Walking down the aisle with a beautiful smile on her face, she sang with the congregation from the open Geneva Psalter.

> "I greet Thee who my sure redeemer art.
> My only Trust and Saviour of my heart.
> Who pain didst undergo for my poor sake;
> I pray Thee from our hearts all cares to take."[32]

On 4 January 1556, young Edward stood beside his father at the baptismal font. Pastor Calvin served as godfather in the sacrament of baptism of the son of Dorothée and Sir William. This ceremony encouraged young couples to look forward to marriage and parenthood in a joyful church community. In nuptials, new members faced each other to take the marriage vows, and they joined hands while kneeling on the prayer bench. They embraced and kissed in public. Within three years, eight marriages and twenty-six baptisms were performed followed by simple social gatherings in the plain sanctuary.[33]

With a sudden beam of light in his face, Calvin, who slept little, stressed, "Man's chief end is to glorify God and to enjoy him forever."[34]

Dorothée's family joined the congregation singing this hymn composed in Geneva:

> "All people that on earth do dwell
> Sing to the Lord with a cheerful voice
> Him serve with mirth, His praises forthtell
> Come ye before Him and rejoice."[35]

Soon after Dorothée's third son was baptized, Sir William Stafford died, and was buried in Geneva. Dorothée, mother of an infant and several young children, faced decisions far beyond her experience. She continued to encourage migration to America, and she sponsored the Protestants Abroad Program.

On 5 June 1559, the great bell Clemence tolled, calling hundreds of students to St. Pierre's Church. When the doors were opened for magistrates to enter, the clergy assembled in a body. All the learned men of Geneva, all the best families of the place, and six hundred scholars were present when Calvin arose, and delivered his speech in French. He advocated the usefulness of educational institutions, and exhorted all who heard him to pray to God for the success of the foundation of an academy.[36]

Calvin, at fifty, habitually preached every day, from week to week, and twice every Sunday, and he lectured on theology three times a week. No earthly power--neither torture nor exile--could persuade him to swerve from the truth. He ate only one meal a day until he became weak and debilitated. Between times Calvin wrote, even at night. His revised *Institutes of Christian Religion* was read to students in the castle by the seigneuress, and her workers distributed this book in homes of peasants.[37]

Dorothée received a royal invitation from her long-time friend, Princess Elizabeth, recently crowned Queen of England. When informed that Queen Mary had died, and the political climate was currently favorable to Protestants, Dorothée packed her collection of Swiss laces, ruffs, and needlepoint embroideries. The few remaining jewels that originally belonged to Catherine of Aragon were tied on the belt around Dorothée's waist when she and her children left Geneva for the long route home to England.

Spelling her name Dorothy Stafford, she returned to the English court in 1562 where was appointed Mistress of the Wardrobe for Queen Elizabeth. During the political policy of peace and recovery, the English liturgy was established, and mass was abolished. A commissioner in the tap room and at gambling tables corrected the behavior of the clergy. Queen Elizabeth, dressed by princess of the wardrobe, Dorothy Stafford, governed as a supreme monarch was supposed to do, while commissioners in the realm nominated bishops who converted offenses and enormities.[38] To support the founding of Protestant colonies abroad, Dorothy contributed money from gems to the Huguenot colony sailing with Rene de Landoniere and John Ribault to Port Royal in the Carolinas. In 1564, she supported another attempted French-English settlement at Fort Caroline, Florida. She studied

Chapter2: Dorothée Stafford

James le Moynes' paintings of Indians that depicted the mode of living of the settlers attacked by Indians. However, these colonies failed. Interest in foreign missions in Virginia prompted Dorothy to invite Rev. Richard Hakluyt who traveled to Virginia, to serve as minister of her parish church in England. She persuaded him to revise and publish a full account of the voyages to Virginia. This appeared in 1584-9 as *Principal Navigations*. Listed were the names of colonists left in Virginia by Sir Richard Grenville.[39] Virginia was thought to extend from Maine to Florida and to the Appalachian Mountains, when Dorothy advised Queen Elizabeth to provide moral and financial support to the early colonists.

In 1589, the Spanish Armada was defeated. Then, the mistress of the queen's wardrobe produced the embroidered taffeta and hand-embroidered ruffs and jewels for Her Majesty to wear when she posed for the Armada Portrait. Dorothy arranged the proper attire for the queen's flirtation with Henry of Anjou, and the Earl of Essex. And, when the foundations of the British navy were laid, she set forth royal regalia for the queen. She remembered the flirtatious manners and dashing appearances of Sir Richard Grenville and the Earl of Cumberland when they were knighted. She prepared for the knighting of Sir Martin Frobisher, Sir John Hawkins, Sir Walter Raleigh, and Sir Francis Drake. Dress was important for meetings with William Cecil, created Lord Burghley in 1570, and Sir Francis Walsingham. Dorothy's son, Sir Edward Stafford, renowned for friendliness to Protestants of all sorts, was appointed ambassador to France. And, she prepared the gown for Queen Elizabeth to meet Sir Francis Knollys, major advisor on the Privy Council, and controller of French wine imported to the queen's household by a royal merchant.

Shortly before her death in 1604, Dorothy urged Bartholomew Gosnold, son of her lawyer, to avoid conflict as vice-admiral and councilor for the Jamestown settlement.[40] Among other associates who met with the queen about exploring America were Sir Henry Knollys, Rev. Richard Hakluyt, and Bartholomew Gosnold.[41] Dorothy repeated Calvin's words, "Your fears will give the enemy the victory which he so greatly desires; we must be aware of his cunning to overcome it . . . Harden yourself, dear (one), against the frown of the world . . . If you do good, this is the reward promised us from above."[42]

The courageous Calvinist spirit of Dorothy Stafford lived on among colonists in the Presbyterian church in Virginia.

Chapter 3
QUEEN JEANNE D'ALBRET
(1528 - June 9, 1572)

Jeanne d'Albret, Queen of Navarre and Bearn, became a Protestant Reformer in the snow-capped Pyrenees Mountains. This daughter of Henry d'Albret, King of Navarre, and Marguerite de Valois-Angouleme, influenced all France by her courage and gallant spirit. Jeanne married Antoine de Bourbon, heir to his father's monarchy and to Bourbon territory in central France. He became King of Navarre. Their son became King Henry IV of France, the most effective of the Bourbon kings. After the Reformation swept through England and Germany like a hurricane, Jeanne encouraged Protestants to colonize America.[1]

While musicians played under sculptured garlands near the fireplace at Fountainebleau Palace, Jeanne, two-year-old niece of Francis I, toddled around the long gallery under the portrait of the monarch and others by Raphael and Leonardo da Vinci. One painting showed Juniper. With her fourteen-year-old cousin in the library, they saw the painting of Juniper carrying off Europa and the Nymph of Fountainebleau. With Mary, daughter of James V of Scotland and Mary of Guise, the child observed the gold and silver treasures, vases, jewelry and gems. On the pavilion, they were exposed to dazzling company at court who believed in the Catholic religion. As she grew, Jeanne was forgiven her sins by the Cardinal of Lorraine.[2] Her mother, Marguerite, sister of Francis I, provided refuge for writers and Protestant ministers at Pau Castle in Navarre. Actually, she kept William Farrell, master of the College of the Cardinal le Moine at Paris, from being burned at stake. Marguerite also defended the Protestant John Calvin who promoted New

Learning. Although Calvin disapproved of the way the queen lived, in defiance of his moral ideas, he was appreciative of being befriended by her in Navarre and Bearn.[3]

The first fifteen years of Jeanne's life were significant. She often travelled from Pau Castle via the royal mail route to Chateau Coarraze. She visited the independent county of Bearn that occupied two-thirds of the Basse-Pyrenees and formed a triangle pointing towards the south of France. From the blind terrace at Pau Castle on the Gave River, Jeanne studied the Haute Pyrenees. The purplish-blue tints in the sky over the mountains attracted her attention until she felt this was an unforgettable gift of God.

Jeanne rode by donkey along the path from the terrace of the Palace at Pau into the piedmont through rising grounds and densely wooded mountains towards the cathedral. At the entrance of Lescar cave, eagles wheeled and screamed when she ducked under the vulture's nest and grape vines, into the pre-historic cavern. She was appalled at the walls containing pictures in the blood of Cro-mangon man, of a bull mounting a cow, and of mountain lions. The drawings of faces of fleeing exiles remained on the limestones beneath the cascading waterfalls flowing over rocks near the cavern. These discoveries left an indelible mark on Jeanne.[4]

About forty kilometers northeastward of the route, four little rivers of the Bay of Biscay--the Gave du Pau, Adour, Garonne and Darre-Basque--merged to form the tributary used by royal merchants to transport glass and cloth to Venice. In this vicinity, Jeanne met the *noblesse de province* considered the backbone of France for so long.[5]

The flag flying over the fortress-castle D'Arricau above forests and fog indicated the baron of Bearn was in residence guarding the House of Bourbon and protecting the Bearnese border from the Spanish. Members of this noble house or "lay abbey," signed names with a fleur-de-lis. Over the fortifications near the mountains of Bearn, the family standard was inscribed, "Death is gain to me." The color gold conveyed the meaning of character and red symbolized valor and courage. One D'Arricau soldier participated in battles with "aux 1 et 4 charge, aux 2 et 3 gueules charge."[6]

Chapter 3: Queen Jeanne d'Albret

The Baron of d'Arricau, while governor of the empire, was not allowed to marry. If convicted of treason, he had the right to be beheaded. He sat in the best pew in church, collected tithes and donated money to musketeers and companions of arms. As a member of the council, he had the right to raise cavalry, to command troops, and to advise the King of Navarre. The baron in the ancient family fortress was reputedly noble "of race and of extraction."[7]

Aristocratic Basques with straight figures and fiercely flashing eyes returned from guild meetings and removed black- fringed cloaks and green sandals. They were proud of antiquities and peculiarities, and kept close to the sentiment of original nobility. They rarely saw the equal in a stranger. In the purest language of Eden, the tongue in which Adam wooed Eve, the nobles who also conversed in Basque, warned, "Never trust Spain whose ruler has stolen by force a large portion of our kingdom of Navarre."[8]

Lands in Bearn had free tenure, and Moors, Jews, and half-caste were not allowed. Near the army confines around the manor, in the parish of D'arricau-Bordes, courageous Bearnese swordsman in the adventurous mood operated the province of Bearn like a small Greek republic.

Jeanne showed a gallant spirit when she married the soldier Antoine de Bourbon, Duke of Vendome and King of Navarre. Relatives present credited the choice of the terrace at Pau Castle, near the Pyrenees, with the success of the ceremony. The sunset on the horizon was an unforgettable gift of God and inspired the bride's sublime grace.

She used her natural eloquence and gift of expression to converse with ministers, and the boldness and courage of the royal bride were appealing. She ignored narrow minded, arrogant civil governors and brazen land-owners because they raised taxes, demanded compulsory services, and caused constant turmoil and fighting. Envious nobles disputed agitating public topics. Some guests resented Queen Catherine d'Medici, and branded as "evil" the late King Francis I.

Jeanne hoped she would never produce a peevish, crying child, and that he would become masculine and vigorous. During the birth of her third son Prince Henry, on 13 December 1553, she sang in the language of Bearn. The monetary value of vineyards to royal families was an important factor in the shaping of France. Therefore, Grandfather rubbed the child's lips with garlic peels dropped in wine from a golden goblet. On the 6th March, the red-haired infant was lifted from his cradle made of tortoise-shells to be baptized a Catholic in the chapel of Pau Castle. He was christened "Prince Henry" by James de Foix, bishop of Lescar.[9]

While pondering how to raise Prince Henry, Jeanne taught him to inhale the perfume of the grape and the mimosa. Stimulated by the sunflowers in the fields, she indicated the violets received the blue from the sky over the Spanish border. She recalled the theories of Protestants such as John Calvin, and the ideas in the Theodore Beza Catechism. These thoughts caused her decision to entrust the care of Prince Henry to Susanne de Bourbon-Busset, wife of Jean d'Albret, Baron de Moissens.

Searching for a place to raise Prince Henry, his mother trudged through the immense stones high in the Pyrenees where she felt the influence of heaven. An ice-ax was used to cut steps to the snow pass to *breche le Roland*. And in the purple-blue mountains, she heard the whooping cry, "Irrincin," that resembled the neighing of a horse, changed to a wolf's howl, and finished with a shake like a jackass's bray.[10] Pure-bred flocks of sheep with distinctive markings of owners were moved by shepherds in black berets who whistled to border collies and followed donkeys on trails into the snow-capped Pyrenees. Bells tinkled from gardens, and fires burned in the old stone huts covered with snow. This countryside appealed to Jeanne as a place for Prince Henry to learn about nature.

From lace-curtained windows in Chateau Coarraze, Jeanne observed pedestrian traffic en route to Lourdes. Sloping piedmont meadows were covered with buttercups, violets, grapes, and apple trees. Lame women searching for John Calvin's form of Christianity, trudged through mountain passes and fled from one Protestant settlement to another. The thick evergreen forests capped in fresh snow were home to wild boar, red deer, owls, and bear.[11]

At Chateau Coarraze, Jeanne departed from her son in light defensive apparel, with explicit orders that he must grow strong. A typical Basque meal included an omelette prepared with tomatoes and green pimentos. According to his taste, onion, garlic, sausage and slivers of ham were added. Other nutritious cuisines included duck, goose pate, fresh fish and the rose wine of France. The prince was given little to eat.[12]

At the chateau, Prince Henry slept on a wooden bed, and was regularly beaten to teach him to cope with the environment. Awakening at the crack of dawn, he was sent into the mountains during the worst weather on fool's errands to study reactions of animals. He tied leather sandals with throngs around his feet, cornered a woolen mantle on his neck, and carried a horn with darts in his hand. With sturdy mountaineers, he rolled and played with dogs until his hair was blanched and his cheeks bronzed. He played pelota with a ball and racquet. He wrestled, pitched quoits at walled courts close to churches, ran, and laughed with friends who had the same innate gaming spirit about swift balls and competition. At neighboring areas, where rights were pass down from hut to hut to erect pigeon nests, a shepherd with a goat on his back caught pigeons in a huge net. Playmates perched in trees with food bags. As the pigeons, at high speed, dove into nets over the gully, the *racquettes* were dropped at impact to avoid injuring the birds.[13] Prince Henry entered the hovels of the poor and conversed with honest mountaineers.

During festival time in Bearn, Jeanne and the prince watched the dance of Zamalzain that represented man's battle with problems of "good" or "evil." The grotesque king of "evil," costumed in rags, believed in good luck for the coming year, and he danced slovenly, toppled the glass, and spilt the red wine. Then the costumed dancer in sandals, with upper body rigid and legs rigid in motion, skimmed above and around the wine glass. When it trembled, he leapt onto the glass, sprang away, and made "good" win out. Sighing, Jeanne applauded approval of beauty triumphing over ugliness, of "good" conquering "evil."[14]

Breakers on the rocky coast prepared Basque fishermen for exploring the American coast. In the time of Francis I, after the voyage of Verrazano to the mouth of the Cape Fear River, France set up a claim in America. The cannon boomed when whaling vessels harpooned a whale. When shipping merchants from England joined the French-English ships at St. Jean-de-Luz, Jeanne joined villagers with drums and tambourines to wave good-bye to Admiral Coligny and his fleet sailing to Newfoundland to form a French empire on the American continent for world trade.[15]

Licensed Bearnese and English dealt in skins such as bear, deer, and mink in Newfoundland. On spring voyages, fishermen in the codfish industry placed their names on wharves in the St. Lawrence River, and participated in whaling at Red Bank, Labrador. Through the English ambassador, free trade was arranged for woolens, wine, and Flemish cloth. And, English exiles in Geneva, such as Sir Francis Russell, had a part in this original plan of colonization.

Since the voyage of Magellan on the La Plata River, Basque fishermen had prepared to explore on the American Coast. And, two of the colony made their way up the La Plata River to Montevideo, the gateway to the riches of Peru.[16] Later, Virginia settlers named property "Montevideo."

In 1555, Villegaman, Knight of Malta, conducted the first French Protestant settlement in Brazil, and Calvin planned to send reinforcements. Huguenot artisans from Geneva followed this plan because the influence of knights was strong. When the chaplain returned from Brazil in 1557, he became minister to Jeanne.[17]

The next year Jeanne, with her husband Antoine, king of Navarre, attended the marriage of Mary Queen of Scots at Notre Dame Cathedral. The royal fleur-de-lis was embroidered on the canopy in front of the church, and the decorations were fantastic. Following the line guards was Francis, duke of Guise, uncle of the bride, and then came Eustace de Bellay, bishop of Paris. Musicians in yellow and red followed, as did a hundred gentlemen-in-waiting who were related princes, and allied bishops, and the cardinals of Bourbon, Lorraine and Guise.

Antoine, king of Navarre, and his two younger brothers led the King--Dauphin Francis. Henry II, and his cousin the duke of Lennox, led his daughter, Mary Stuart, whose mother was in Scotland. The happy, beautiful, and graceful bride was dressed in a robe white as lilies, and her golden crown was garnished with precious stones.

Jeanne, queen of Navarre, had brought her six-year-old son, the future Henry IV. At one of several balls following a banquet, the king of Navarre danced with Princess Elizabeth. After the ball the entire court proceeded through the crowds to

Chapter 3: Queen Jeanne d'Albret

the palace of the parliament, the gentlemen on horseback, the ladies in litters. At this ball the king of Navarre chose his wife, Jeanne d'Albret, to dance. Many of the group on display were strange due to the fact that most husbands brought wives from abroad. Antoine, among those who realized France was bankrupted by the struggle against the Empire and Italians, whispered of opposition to the Guise marriage to the Venetian ambassador.[18]

In 1559 at Pau Castle in Navarre, Jeanne, with her husband Antoine, King of Navarre and Bearn, became aware of the influence of Protestants in exile. The queen welcomed displaced Huguenots from Bearn and Navarre who fled to the English coast in search of a better life when the political situation was changing. Prices were exorbitant, and life was immoral. And, Francis Duc de Guise and Cardinal Lorraine, uncles of King Francis II, controlled the finances of the French government. Jeanne associated knowledge with faith when she joined the recently established Protestant church countenanced by the King of Navarre in 1560. The Protestant nobles of the States General contributed to churches in towns, to support teachers for the instruction of children. And, the primary school was the child of Protestantism.[19]

Although Prince Henry had taken the oath to observe the Orthodox religion, and attended mass with his father in July 1561, Jeanne accompanied the nine-year-old to the Court of France. His instruction in Protestantism had begun. That Christmas his mother abjured Catholicism, publicly took communion, and sent the nine-year-old on a journey through the kingdom.[20]

During the wars of Protestants against Catholics, Jeanne worried because her husband, Antoine, Lieutenant-General of the Kingdom, was forbidden to trade with the Spanish Indies. With the chevaliers, he sang the first epic poem in France, *Chanson de Roland*, hundreds of times, and trumpets blasted. He rode sturdy horses among Frankish counts in leather coats studded with iron discs. Their wooden shields were covered with leather, and they carried a sword, short hurling lances, and a double-headed battle-axe. As the result of wounds received at war during the siege of Rouen, Antione de Boubourn died on 17 November 1562. On his death bed, he had repented these wars. Saddened by his death, his wife's mind was affected with quarrels of religion within her family.[21] The Queen of Navaree proclaimed herself an advocate of the Huguenot party. Prince Henry was enrolled in educational classes at the Old College of Navarre that was attached to the University of Paris, and distinguished by royal favor.[22]

Jeanne supported Coligny's plan to help the homeless form a French-English settlement in 1562 under Protestant Jean Ribault. This pupil of mathematician John Dee established Fort Charles--now Port Royal, South Carolina. However, the colonists returned to France the next year. In 1564, Queen Jeanne sponsored another English-French settlement on the St. John's River near St. Augustine, Florida, under Rene Laudonnier. And, John Calvin and Sir Francis Knollys promised to send a second supply. After Calvin's death, Jeanne sent supplies with Sir Edward Horsey and Sir Henry Sidney to Fort Caroline on the River May, Florida. These immigrants were massacred by Spain, "not as Frenchmen but as Lutherans." Both colonies had been annihilated.[23]

In 1563, the courageous Queen publicly proclaimed the reformed religion in her kingdom. She made wisdom and goodness welcome without distinction of creed throughout southern Europe. Calvinism had spread into southern France. When French women undertook arduous labors, they fought side by side on walls, and helped repair beaches at night. And more women were killed than men. Because Jeanne inherited her mother's good virtues, her courage sustained the Huguenots through the struggle. In Bearn, a divine service, including the Apostles' Creed, was regularly performed, and the Lord's Supper was administered with bread and wine. As long as the congregations would listen, Jeanne taught prayers of her own devising and preached from pulpits in Huguenot churches with all her heart. Using the Roman Catholic ritual she never prayed for archbishops and bishops, only for the Queen. Open to charges of suspicion, and at the mercy of those who heard her, a queen was not a qualified minister. Jeanne prepared the army to defend the beliefs of the Protestant Gospel. This was her instrument of instilling the soldiers and sailors in Bearn and Navarre with the spirit of order.[24]

Public prayers were held morning and evening. There were no indelicate songs, only the Psalms of David. Crimes were promptly revealed, and no blasphemy was heard. No lewd women were among the camp followers. Thefts were infrequent and vigorously punished. Jeanne taught equality of all men before God. The Protectress of the Protestant party publicly proclaimed the reformed religion in her kingdom.[25]

Adolescent Prince Henry was surrounded with teachers of high mental and moral attainments in Protestantism. And he was exposed to the beliefs of the hospitalers organized to care for the poor and strangers. The Maltese Cross, white on a red background, represented cardinal virtues to the knights under the protection of the Bourbon kings. The Knights of St. John, known as hospitalers, considered the world their field to be ploughed. In Rhodes, and later in Valetta, Malta, the city of knights with a governor converted to Christianity, was a crossroads of the Mediterranean, a bridge between Europe and Africa. In a hostel with an ancient church and a defense tower at Irissary in Bass-Navarre, and in Soule, the prince learned the meanings of this eight-pointed cross and was prepared to become the only Protestant King of France.[26] At age thirteen, Prince Henry abandoned rough manners, moderated his language, and acted like he had turned eighteen at the royal court at Chateau de Nerac. After hunting, playing tennis, and fencing, Prince Henry exchanged his plain country clothes for satin doublets, breeches, and silk stockings. His velvet hat was decked with feathers, and a scarlet cloak with gold and silver embroidery. On farms and cottages near woodlands full of game, Protestants and Catholics lived peacefully in luxuriously decorated castles. When Prince Henry returned to Pau, he knew Latin and spoke Latin, French, Spanish, and Italian. He had learned about the history of France, and read works of Plutarch.[27]

In 1567, after the Pope issued an official bull of excommunication against Jeanne because of her heresy, she returned to Paris. Near her castle in La Rochelle, she promoted printing presses and endowed a French college. Here, Huguenots set fire to monasteries and farms, and made Catholics hand over gold. Pieces of gold and silver from sacred vases and relics stolen at Orleans were minted. Subjected to these wicked ways of court, Prince Henry became disillusioned about his mother's associates, and he had encounters with the Basque nobility.[28] Jeanne attended a hunt near a castle in northern France with Prince Henry and a few of her court.

However, she separated her group from the chase of foxes, and turned the heads of horses towards Pau Castle, and they traveled homeward day and night in relays.

Jeanne had left news carriers in the French court, and returned to Pau, where Prince Henry, Lieutenant-General of the Kingdom of Navarre, had his first encounters with the Basque nobility. In La Rochelle, Jeanne handed Prince Henry over to her aristocratic brother-in-law, Louis de Bourbon, Prince de Condé, head of the Protestant army. The aristocratic element furnished military leadership to the Protestants. Ambassador Henry Sidney offered this group thousands of soldiers and horses to guard each city under the Duke of Condé, leader at Orleans.[29] When the Prince of Conde's horse was killed under him and he could not extricate himself, Jeanne's Protestant faith became obvious by her words, "Our conclusion is that he died on the true bed of honor both for body and soul, for the service of his God and the king and the spirit of his fatherland."[30]

Jeanne escorted the eldest son of the Prince of Condé and sixteen-year-old Prince Henry to Cognac. Holding the hands of these lads, the Queen addressed the soldiers assembled, "My friends, we weep the loss of the Prince of Condé, who supported with courage and fidelity the party. . .I offer you my son, the young prince of Bearn; (and) I confide . . . (the) son of the prince . . . Heaven grant that they may both prove themselves worthy inheritors of the valor of their ancestors and that the sight of these tender pledges may unceasingly urge you to continue united for the maintenance of the cause you defend."[31]

Prince Henry immediately stepped forward like a soldier, and was proclaimed commanding general. Some thought the greatest leaders of the Calvinists were the ladies, and Queen Jeanne. During the wars of religion when more women were killed than men, the Queen joined women of all ranks to share the toils.

In 1570, Admiral Gaspard de Coligny, invested with command under Prince Henry, was successful at Rabasteins garrison at the foot of the Pyrenees and moved towards Toulouse. After the massacre by students in the Toulouse law school that ancient, walled city, was thrown into the hands of Huguenots. During carnage and riots, the Protestant leader was killed. The fierce passions of people of Bearn were

Chapter 3: Queen Jeanne d'Albret 35

unreconciled to the edict of peace.[32]

In spite of Huguenot leaders fighting for their religion in wild guerilla warfare, the Queen, trying to be honest and faithful, did everything she could to stop the fury. The gold medal presented to the chief was inscribed with her own seal and that of her son. This stated, "certain peace, complete victory, or noble death." Bearnese nobles and peasants were urged to come to the Protestant camp she directed, where shooting dice was wicked, and playing games of chance was gambling. The queen promoted calisthenics, with good nutrition, and among the followers of Calvin, she breathed deeply, swinging her arms. She prayed for a peaceful spirit and fined herself every time she forgot to pray.[33] Close to the Bearnese mint on the Gave, Jeanne protested with intelligence, courage and strength near the guillotine. The Catholic soldiers rioted, killed, and attempted ferocious assaults. On the other side of the area, churches and convents were burned. On 4 March 1571, when mass was abolished upon pain of death, priests were thrown out of the window at Orthey bridge. At Pau, the lords who surrendered on pretext of safety were disavowed by the Queen, and their punishment was severe.[34]

In 1571, lay elders in churches approved the Protestant idea of connecting canals throughout France so the *famille bourgeoisie* could enjoy privileges of aristocrats. The Queen ordered a Protestant version of the New Testament printed at La Rochelle during the "paper war."[35] Prince Henry, supported by Bearnese musketeers and swordsmen from fortress d'Arricau, appreciated the courage and adventurous spirit of the Basque nobility in the French army. Friends coined and donated money to his valiant companions at arms and to his musketeers.[36] When Prince Henry sojourned at Bearn in the ninth French provincial synod, lay elders pledged support of Protestants from fifteen or more churches. There were more Huguenots led by men of mark than papists.[37]

On March 4, 1572, Jeanne refused to agree that Margaret of Valois be guaranteed permission to celebrate mass in Pau. The area was cleared of a corrupt society. Concerned about the marriage of Prince Henry to Margaret of Valois, Jeanne refused to consent that her son and his bride should reside at a royal court without exercising his own religion. Jeanne had cleansed the district of Bearn of idolatry.³⁸

In June 1572, at Blois Chateau Jeanne met Catherine d'Medici, the bride's mother, to plan the wedding of Prince Henry to Margaret Valois. According to an agreement, Henry would receive a large dowry, the marriage was not to take place in the church, and the groom would not attend mass. However, Margaret was granted permission to celebrate mass in Bearn, although Jeanne knew this could prove the ruin of her friends and their lands.³⁹

Jeanne wrote to Prince Henry, "(The Lady Margaret) is handsome, modest and graceful, but nurtured in the most wicked, corrupt society that ever was. I have not seen a person who does not show the effects of it. . .I would not for the world that you were here to live. It is on this account that I want you to marry, and your wife and you to come out of this corruption. . . . Were you here, you would never escape but by. . .God's mercy. I abide by my first opinion: that you must return to Bearn."⁴⁰ Jeanne was firm in trials of adversity, and she was zealous and liberal.

In the Paris lodgings of Catherine d'Medici, Jeanne was seized with a fever that lasted nine days. While in an ordinary bed without candles or priests, crucifix or holy water, she said, "God will be their father and protector, as he has been mine in my greatest afflictions."

During the fever, it is said that the forty-year-old Queen of Navarre drew on a glove supposedly filled with a deadly poison from the queen mother's library drawers. She died with a fever, on June 9, 1572.⁴¹

Eight Protestant ministers attended the funeral, and Jeanne's mansion was a regular asylum for Calvinist preachers. The soldiers Walter Raleigh and Edward Horsey hastened across the English Channel to secure the crown of Navarre for Prince Henry.⁴²

The Great Protestant Reformer Jeanne, Protectress of the Protestant Party, was dead in June, as was her friend Condé. And, in August 1572, Coligny was killed. The Maltese Cross on Jeanne's tombstone indicated her international goodwill towards the Knights of St. John. They stood valiantly for Christianity. Jeanne had joined kings and queens contributing to the international Order of St. John, composed of military knights of nobility, chaplains, and serving brothers.

Chapter 3: Queen Jeanne d'Albret

And, the Queen had rejoiced in the news she received from Venice that the Christian fleet had won a decisive victory over the Turkish fleet at the Gulf of Lepanto. The sentiments of this Queen were divulged in her will, "God will honor those who honor him, dishonor those who dishonor him."[43]

Jeanne reigned with Calvinist severity and had a first place in the religious annals and politics of France in the sixteenth century. She was firm in trials of adversity, and she was zealous and liberal. Her hoped-for settlements in Brazil, Paris Island, and Florida failed. After her son, Henry IV, was forced to take up the Catholic religion again, he became "the greatest king France ever had."[44]

Chapter 4
MARY QUEEN OF SCOTS
(1542-February 1587)

Mystery surrounded the plots concerning Mary Queen of Scots. The ideas stirred by religious groups in Scotland included the Queen's Men with Protestant affiliations and her Roman Catholic sympathizers. Her political situation in Scotland extended to England, France, and Italy. After Mary married her cousin, Lord Darnley, a child of the Earl of Lennox who owned the Dukedom of Rich Mond, a King's Party was formed.

Mary became a queen before she was a week old. The daughter of James V of Scotland and his second wife, Mary of Guise-Lorraine, was born at her father's birthplace and favorite residence, Linlithgow Palace on the Firth of Forth. Half French in temperament, Mary was one of the proud, bold Guises, and during her first years in Scotland, she learned to speak in Scottish.

After her father died, Mary, age six, was sent to France, and she corresponded in French about private matters. Brought up to marry Henry VIII's frail son Prince Edward, in England, she excelled in needlework, gardening, and horsemanship. In musical concerts, she played the harpsichord and flute. In the luxurious surroundings at Fountainbleau Palace that included golden doors and tapestries used by Eleanor of Austria, she wore gorgeous pearls. She loved to dance with the king. And, her sins were forgiven by her uncle, Cardinal of Lorraine, a Guise.[1]

At age sixteen, Mary married the little Dauphin, Francis, eldest son of the King of France, on 24 April 1558, in the Cathedral of Notre Dame. Upon the death of the French king on 20 July 1559, Mary's feeble husband Francis II was called to the throne. Aided by her good friends Diane de Poitiers and Lady Fleming, the queen showed painful devotion in her godly voice to Francis II during his sickness and death on 5 December 1560. Relieved of the crown of France, his widow Mary had little hope of recovering her sole patrimony and dower from her mother--the crown of Scotland.[2]

After the death of Francis II, Mary received little consolation. Hopeful of inspiring pity from courtiers, she brooded over her disasters with constant tears and doleful lamentations. Cardinal Stewart advised Mary to leave France, and to avoid Huguenot ships. Leaving Brittany and the magnificent courts of France for sparsely settled Scotland, one ship in Mary's fleet passed through English waters with horses, mules, and supplies. She sailed without the acknowledgement of a passport, a legal necessity issued by the Privy Council of Queen Elizabeth. Refusing food, and resting both arms on the rail of the great galley, Mary shed floods of tears. She demanded her bed be prepared on deck. In the morning she boldly spoke, "Farewell, France! I think I shall never see thee more!"[3]

Before the Queen arrived in Scotland, she was compelled to renounce her claim to the English throne. And, she had to ratify the Act of the Scottish Parliament, which forbade the performance of Holy mass, under pain of death. When her mother had ruled the Scottish region, and supported the civil war with French forces, Scotland was declared a Protestant nation. The lords and earls had mixed antecedents, outlooks and motives.

Arriving in August 1561, Mary was conveyed from Leith Row to Holyrood Palace amid music and bonfires that expressed the joy of crowds in Edinburgh. A Holy mass took place at the chapel of Holyrood Palace on her first Sabbath. Afterwards, companies of men made the statement that they could not abide a reintroduction of the Catholic mass.[4]

The open-minded queen sought a knowledge of God in a land ruled by regents and commissioners. Presbyterianism was established, and she surrounded herself with Protestant advisers. When she insisted upon a free mass for all Catholics and Protestants, the reception of this policy led to turmoil. John Knox, a Scottish Protestant lately returned from Geneva, helped six ministers establish the

Chapter 4: Mary Queen of Scots
41

Confession of Faith, ratified by Parliament as the "infallible word of God." This confession, a miraculous deliverance from the civil war, used the key words "cleave, serve, worship, and trust," reflecting a spirit of trust and commitment to God.[5]

Knox criticized the eighteen-year-old queen's lifestyle when she rode by, and he denounced "the stinking pride of women." Dressed in embossed silks with pearls, Mary had a massive hair arrangement held in place with jewels. The diamonds she wore were gifts of Henry II, or Diane of France, and her enameled broaches had sacred scenes. When brow-beaten by Knox, the beautiful queen shed tears, became hard-hearted, and yielded to masterful men. Mary was the center of intrigue among Scots whose Gaelic ancestors were from southern Ireland.[6] In lace and gold and velvet, trying to charm the people and win them to restore the old faith, the queen spoke in Scottish.

She rode through the gate of St. Giles' Church where the London Prayer Book was read. Behind houses were gardens, green fields, and woods surrounded by lakes. Monastic structures and churches lay in ruins, due to English invaders and reformed religious services. Burgesses, tradesmen, and artisans gathered with nobles at Cowgate Palace and Canongate Presbyterian Kirk. From windows, burgesses handed spears to friends. A fiery mob could defend their May-day sport of Robin Hood against the preachers and Bible-loving middle classes. Broils were common near the stake where husbands were burned, and there was a pillory for a Catholic priest. At the base of Castle Cliff, fornicators were ducked on the Norloch in pits full of trout. On town gate spikes were heads of those who sinned against the law. Passing ruins where monks had lived, labored, and manuscripts were burned, Mary saw a gallows tree, and fallen troops of gallants and girls. Tall buildings were in the skyline near Holyrood Abbey towers. The extinct volcanic peak, Arthur's Seat, was to the north. As the queen passed landmarks, masters of sheep dogs shouted, "Heaven bless that sweet face!"[7]

With Scottish patriots, she left St. Margaret's Chapel in Edinburgh Castle, where the honors of Scotland and the insignia of royalty were housed. Sometimes at mid-night, masked in male apparel, she added spice to festival groups singing Gaelic ballads. She joined dancers in kilts and passed those tasting soups and haggis along the streets of red-roofed, unsanitary Edinburgh. Mary at times played cards and chess.[8]

The documented fact that the Queen of Scots was of the same lineage as Elizabeth, Queen of England, was paramount. Of utmost importance was the understanding with Elizabeth that Mary and her issue should be recognized as heirs to the English throne. Mary's political rivalry was of great concern to politicians, and she agreed to their general policy of governing. In accordance with the advice received in France, she hoped for toleration from the Catholics remaining in exile in England. Although Scotsmen refused to endure a restoration of the Catholic Church, property owners, such as the Lennox family, continued to maintain the abodes they had owned before the religious turmoil. Mary worked to maintain her peace with the English, and her succession to that throne remained under scrutiny. Thirteen days after her return to Scotland, Mary sent Elizabeth the message of her safe arrival.[9]

Mary created her brother James, natural son of James V, the Earl of Moray (Murray). This chief Protestant minister in Scotland, a warrior, and sometimes a traitor, had territorial rivalries across the country. For this favor, he presented his sister an antidote ring. This was supposed to counteract the effects of poison and to contain magical properties to burn witches.[10]

After Sir Henry Sidney informed Mary in Holyrood that her interview with Elizabeth must be deferred for a year, she undertook a long journey. She accompanied her brother, the Earl of Moray, and his soldiers to the North where Lord Huntly had offered to restore the queen by force, and with her, the Catholic church. At Huntly Palace the queen's group defeated him, her chief Catholic supporter, known as "Cock of the North," and the castle was plundered. Huntly, dead after battle, fell off his horse. Later, the queen approved the execution of one of his sons who supported the warlike Scots of the Border. The Protestants regained substantial advantages after her journey.[11]

The chief scout, Lord Lieutenant of Argyll, was in the queen's company when she went to the Kirk in the Field. The Argylls were the only West Highland magnates regularly immersed in national affairs. Their ancestral lands bordered on

Chapter 4: Mary Queen of Scots 43

the Firth of Clyde, within easy reach of the central Lowlands. And, off Duarte Point, Lady's Rock was the scene of dramatic incidents during clan warfare. In stormy weather the high tide splashed over this isolated rock and the mainland. In the Sound of Mull, a home of the Macleans, Duarte Castle had 15 feet-thick curtain walls, and a tremendous tower.[12]

Mary sought a remedy in France that would allow her to assert her rights in England and Scotland. Her mother's list of principal men in the nation, and their politics, helped the widow determine the best suitor. If she married Don Carlos, the Emperor of Austria, the continuance of amnesty between Mary and Elizabeth would be impossible. If she married to Elizabeth's satisfaction, this queen of England would be a friend, and might make Mary heir to the throne. Courtiers suggested suitable husbands such as Lord Robert Dudley, or the Duke of Orleans, or Charles IX. Also mentioned was the King of Sweden, his brother, the King of Denmark, the King of Navarre, the Duke of Ferrara. Mary studied characteristics of the Prince of Condé, the Duke of Orleans (afterwards Henry the Third), the young Duke of Guise, the Cardinal of Bourbon, Don John, Ferdinand, a son of Geoffrey Pole's, and the Duke of Norfolk.[13]

In 1564, the queen became engaged to her spoiled cousin Henry Stuart, later Lord Darnley. His own claim to the English succession could strengthen Mary's, and his parents were practicing Catholics. Although disliked by the Earl of Argyll, this child of the Earl of Lennox, was "a comely Prince of fair and large stature, pleasant in countenance. . .as well exercised in martial pastimes upon horseback as any Prince of that age." As great-grandson of Henry VII, and cousin of Mary Stuart, he might unite the two crowns of England and Scotland. Despite his charming manners, he had a girlish bloom, and was sometimes arrogant, violent, and forgetful. According to rumor, he drew his jeweled dagger, and insulted an official who brought a disappointing message. Bystanders were alarmed at the way Darnley spoke to Murray. The queen acted like a new character when she was smitten by the power of love for her handsome cousin whose favorite amusements were tennis and exercising horses. Because of his peevish disposition and addiction to medicines the queen was blinded and confused about whether to encourage him or cool the friendship.[14]

At six o'clock in the morning, on 29 July 1565, clothed in mourning in memory of King Francis II, Mary, Queen of Scots, married Henry Stewart, Lord Darnley. The ceremony was celebrated with great significance at massive Holyrood Palace. The couple promised the Pope to defend the Catholic religion to the utmost of their power. As far as religion was concerned, the royal couple had the liberty to live as they wished in the marriage union made for the sake of Darnley. From Glasgow, and from Dumbarton House on the Firth of Clyde where Mary Fleming, the queen's favorite attendant lived, a raven followed the couple. The same bird remained perched on the roof of Darnley's house in Kirk o' Field.[15]

When the Gaels, on a slope behind, signaled a serious insurrection in Scotland, the queen summoned help from secretary James Hepburn, Earl of Bothwell, in France. He had espoused the cause of Mary of Guise against the Protestant lords of the Congregation. His masterful nature attracted women at the French court, where it was rumored he had three wives simultaneously. In mid-September, he cast a spell over the queen of Scotland. Some nobles there accused him of trying to win her favor by witchcraft. Although Bothwell was outlawed, the queen favored him, and kept him to be a soldier. True to the queen's disposition, she became familiar with him. Added to her problems with her opponents was their jealousy of her secretary for French affairs, David Ricco, an Italian musician.[16]

The queen's estrangement from Darnley began because he wished his father would be chosen to govern the Border, and she gave this post to the Earl of Bothwell. Darnley's adversaries were secretly encouraged by Queen Elizabeth to assemble in arms during the crushing of Murray's revolt in October 1565. After a rebellion, Murray, the Hamiltons and Argyll were driven into England, where they became harmless, and this action precipitated the ill-feeling between Darnley, Bothwell, and Argyll.

Prior to the rebellion, Riccio, the queen's chief associate, was a court favorite who assisted her at Holyrood Palace. Politicians hinted she was in love with secretary Riccio. Rebel lords complained Riccio, a foreign upstart and a Roman Catholic emissary of the Pope, plotted to overthrow their religion. They did not

Chapter 4: Mary Queen of Scots 45

assume he was a lover of Mary. Her husband was persuaded Riccio was the real obstacle to his designs upon the crown. Because relations with the queen were tense, Darnley and his father, the Earl of Lennox, competitors for the Scottish crown, complained to the Council about the situation. This group accused her husband Darnley of extortions at Glasgow. Outraged and harassed, he agreed with the belief that the queen favored Bothwell. When the queen suddenly altered her love of Darnley, the king, and excluded him from Council affairs, he took to the field to hunt and hawk. The queen's love cooled.[17]

Without Darnley's consent, she granted a pardon to rebels named Hamilton, and the couples' estrangement began. This measure was distasteful to Darnley and the Earl of Lennox, who had been feuding with the Hamiltons over the heir to the Scottish crown. They planned for the pardon of Murray and others who were not Hamiltons. The December pardon attributed to Riccio, brought humiliation and five years of exile. Because Mary, then pregnant, expected an offspring from her marriage to Darnley, the Lennox party could not accuse her of a guilty, amorous affair before mid-November 1565. In Sterling Castle, her health was failing and she was subject to fainting fits. Her enemies claimed the queen dressed in homely attire in the Market Place.[18]

Darnley entered into a formal compact known as a "Band of Assurance for the Murder" that included Murray, Ruthven, Morton and other chiefs of the Protestant party. Lords, barons, freeholders, gentlemen, merchants and craftsmen assisted in the plan. The queen faced the chance that certain great persons would be slain in her presence, or within Holyrood House. She could die of shock, and would be morally disgraced. The result of this conspiracy was the murder of Riccio by Bothwell's group. A Huntly broke into Mary's room and slew Riccio on 5 March 1566.[19]

The queen, who had seen him dead, became ill from this murder. Sir William Cecil in England heard her foes tell the lie that Riccio had been slain in Mary's arms, and friends on the Borders in the North and South fought their way to assist her. Her council advised Mary, for health reasons, to play golf at Seton. There, in the darkness of her room, with courage and amazing coolness, she received an English envoy and had someone speak for her.[20]

Before the tragedy, the queen made a match for Bothwell with Lady Jane Gordon, a Catholic, and she gave the wedding dress to the bride. That marriage took place in the Protestant Kirk of Canongate Palace, and the honeymoon was interrupted by the happenings pertaining to the queen. While sick with episodes of fainting, she tried to keep Murray and other nobles apart from the displaced king, and she suspected an intrigue whenever they conversed.

Mary's friends from away, overpowered by numbers, sought their apartments. When the attempt was made to reconcile them to the situation, they escaped at night, and the company dissolved. Once more she demanded the pardon of those who insulted and injured her by the murder of her servant Riccio, and she boldly exposed herself to penalties in hope of a victory. About this event she wrote, "We could never forget it."[21]

She hated Darnley and all his kin, and repented her marriage. Before her child's birth, she offered to divorce him, and advised him to take a mistress, ". . .and I assure you I shall never love you the worse." Fearful of death, she made an inventory for bequests of her jewels including the red enamel wedding ring with which he married her. She secretly communicated with Bothwell and Huntly to arrange a plan for her flight by means of ropes let down from the windows of Edinburgh Castle, and the passage through the basement into the royal tombs. With aid, she made her way to Dunbar Castle. The renowned Protestant John Knox fled from the Kirk o' Field and Edinburgh and found refuge in England. When Darnley betrayed his accomplices, she was left to reconcile Murray and Argyll to Huntly, Bothwell, and Atholl. Mary Fleming held Dumbarton Castle while the queen lingered abed and received company.[22]

At twenty-three, ill, and almost dead, the queen gave birth to her son Prince James of Scotland on 19 June 1566, probably in the queen's Chamber in the Exchequer House of Edinburgh Castle. The great rejoicing and many bonfires brightened Edinburgh. People gathered in St. Giles' Church to thank God for the honor of having an heir to their kingdom. Some Scots claimed Mary lowered the royal infant in a basket from the castle to the narrow street to be baptized a Catholic

Chapter 4: Mary Queen of Scots

and to escape the clutches of Protestant reformers.[23]

Huge amounts of money were spent on the celebration of the baptism of James VI of Scotland on 17 December 1566 at Stirling Castle where there was strict security. Ambassadors of France and England came to the cradle bearing a font of enamelled gold, a gift from cousin Queen Elizabeth, the child's godmother. Pageants, fireworks, and festivals ensued. Chanting choirs sang about Queen Mary's crowns of Virtue and of Royalty. After the queen won permission for this rite, Catholic ecclesiastics in splendid attire baptized the child. The tall queen was recognized by the color of her hair, or periwig, and the mysterious hairstyle remained. Her task was to quiet Scotland that was upset over the revolution in religion and in politics.

Darnley, the child's father, although under guard in Sterling Castle, failed to attend the baptism of his son. He had departed two days before with grandfather Lennox for Glasgow Castle. Darnley had been warned, after the christening and departure of the ambassadors, that he might be apprehended and put in a ward. He postponed seeing his child until the triumph was over and ambassadors left Scotland. Darnley fell sick at Glasgow.[24]

After her deliverance, the queen almost drove her husband and Murray to fatal dagger strokes. She and Murray conversed often. And, she told Murray that Darnley was determined to kill him. The king, weaving new intrigues, resented the queen's use of familiar approaches with men and women. After her fear of childbirth disappeared, she disliked Darnley because his kinsmen were likely to put their hands in his blood. He was in constant pain and under sedation. The fateful plot of the lords playing dice around Darnley's couch in his crowded sick room in Kirk o' Field included Murray, Argyll, Huntly, Lethington, and Bothwell. Under the flare of torches down the Blackfrairs Wynd, the queen rode on to Holyrood Palace.[25]

Accompanied by the Protestant Murray, she galloped from her secure stone house in Jedburgh through the land of robbers to Hermitage Castle. She hastened to Craigsmiller Castle near Edinburgh with her infant. Her energies surpassed those of the picked guards in her company. She galloped back the same day from the towerhouse to visit her wounded lover, the Earl of Bothwell, near the Border. She bestowed on him the command of her new Guard, consisting of a wild crew of mercenaries under dare-devil captains. She allowed him to rule her court. Her gratitude and confidence turned to love. In July-August 1567 she secretly fled from Edinburgh with Bothwell to Alloa, and gave him a magnificent bed and a quantity of cloth of gold. She united with the band to resist Lord Darnley's authority, although she said nothing about violence. In her chamber in the Exchequer House in Edinburgh, she was betrayed into Bothwell's hands, where he overcame her virtue by force. So began their tragic loves.[26]

The queen succumbed to fear and courageously took to the fields herself. She endured misunderstandings over her lands, the murder of a court favorite, and Bothwell's unsavory divorce. She heard the shrill sound and drum roll as pipers in kilts with bagpipes performed.[27]

Her triumph was scarcely over when misunderstanding began to arise between her and her husband. She had given Darnley the title of king, but he now demanded the crown should be secured to him for life. If the queen died without issue, the crown should descend to his heirs. By neglecting the Earl of Lennox and Darnley, and by his jealousy of Riccio, the queen had incurred the feud with the English Stuarts. Darnley had been full of mad projects, including a scheme for kidnapping Prince James, whereby he aimed to seize the child, to crown him, and rule in his name.[28]

On Sunday night, 9 February 1567, on the eve of the explosion near the decayed town wall of Kirk o' Field, Darnley lay sick in one small room of their two-story house. The accommodations were furnished with magnificent tapestries and a velvet bed inherited from Mary of Guise. The day before the tragic happening, the queen visited Darnley while he was writing, and she kissed him. After singing Psalm V to his servants, he drank to them, and went to bed. He died that night.[29]

His lifeless body was found in the neighboring garden. The same raven was heard croaking on the roof! One theory was that the Darnley house was razed from the ground by a train of powder such as a mine. Some thought he was first strangled in a low stable by a wet napkin steeped in vinegar and thrust into his mouth. Another theory was that he fled from the house when he heard the key of the

Chapter 4: Mary Queen of Scots 49

murderers grate in the keyhole. Clad in a shirt and carrying his dressing gown, he was followed, and dragged into a little area outside his own wall where the queen used to play music and sing in the garden of Kirk o' Field.[30] Some said the queen appeared at the funeral of her husband in the man's apparel she loved to wear when dancing secretly with the king.[31]

In this tragedy the chief actor was undoubtedly Bothwell. Since Murray's revolt, and still more since Riccio's murder, Bothwell had enjoyed a large share of the queen's favor. When the earl was brought to a mock-trial, and acquitted on 12 April 1567, some suspected the queen herself was not wholly ignorant of the plot to murder Darnley. When this case was inquired into at Westminster, Mary's notes claimed that over thirty or forty men were involved.[32]

In hope of victory, Mary exposed herself to many perils near Stirling Castle on the River Forth at the gateway to the Highlands, where she loved to handle the cords of a ship and habitually travelled by sea. The ancient castle of volcanic rock was surrounded by beautiful gardens on level slopes, and tournaments were held on the meadows. With secretary Lethington, she approached through the gate house towers and a wall into the great hall of ancient Stirling Castle. On this visit to her son James VI, on 21 April 1567, Mary thought of poison, because there was a web of intrigue of men in the clans of the Lennox family. On the 23rd April she went to Linlithgow, and on the 24th, Bothwell, with a large force, seized her and her protectors at a place close to Edinburgh, and carried her to his stronghold at Dunbar on the Firth of Forth. Lennox was fleeing aboard ship on the west coast. When the queen saved Bothwell's life, he divorced his wife of a year, but continued to court her. Later, many were arrested including the Archbishop and a priest.[33]

If the queen married Bothwell, she would ruin her secretary's project of uniting the crowns of England and Scotland on Mary or her child. Bothwell loathed Prince James. The queen's remaining supporters witnessed her wretchedness, when she called out for a knife to slay herself. Her face changed, and some prophesied she would be burned when she had five husbands. She feared the same. She concealed no cowardice. Her defenders attributed her sorrow to the gloom of a captive forced into a hated wedlock. On 15 May 1567 Mary married

Bothwell in the old chapel of Holyrood Palace, a great hall where the Council used to sit. He was "beastly suspicious and jealous."[34]

The queen's confessor protested that her marriage with Bothwell was illegal. Despite remonstrances of an envoy to France to denounce the Protestant preacher, Mary hurried through the double process of divorce. To sooth preachers, Bothwell attended sermons. The queen proclaimed herself a free agent, and created him Duke of Orkney, and his land was located in the far north. She was miserable.[35]

When lords banded together and appealed to Queen Elizabeth for help, she hesitated. Mary invited herself to dinner with her reluctant subjects. The golden font, the christening gift of Elizabeth, was melted down and coined for pay to the guard of musketeers on 31 May 1568. Her secretary Lethington fled to the lords, and the next day Mary and Bothwell retired to Bothwick Castle. When he fled to Dunbar four days later, Mary sent a proclamation bidding the citizens to arm and free her, not from Bothwell, but from the lords.

The queen fled to Dunbar in male apparel, and Bothwell met her on 13 June 1567. They mustered forces. Lethington, whose life she had preserved, and cohorts at the head of 200 horse surrendered Edinburgh Castle. When the lords entered the town, Mary bid the commander of the castle to fire on them. When he disobeyed, this was a deadly stroke at the queen. The next day, Bothwell slipped away to Dunbar Palace and took the queen clad in a "red petticoat, sleeves tied with points, a velvet hat and muffler."[36]

Later, when Mary wished her marriage with Bothwell to be annulled, the Protestant lords refused assent, and she was forced to surrender to them at Carberry Hill. Bothwell escaped capture. In June 1567, with the Queen of Scots a captive in their hands, the lords needed some better excuse than her obstinate adherence to the husband whom they had selected for her. For their conduct that would have a retroactive effect, they needed a reason--the positive proof of her guilt of murder.[37]

The fatal step at once arrayed her nobles in arms against her. She was able to lead an army against them, but it melted away without striking a blow on the field of Carberry. On 15th of June nothing was left to the queen but to abandon Bothwell and surrender herself to the confederate lords. Mary was imprisoned the next day.

Chapter 4: Mary Queen of Scots

On the 21st they proclaimed they knew the whole secret of Mary's guilt.[38]

They issued a summons against Bothwell for Darnley's murder. Under the queen's name and her signet, this stated, "for taking the Queen's most noble person by force to her Castle of Dunbar, detaining her, and for fear of her life making her promise to marry him." Some lords in the Council engaged in preaching and in common prayer. They had confessed to the murder and verified that they banded with Bothwell to enable him to marry Mary. Some were spreading the rumor of Mary's wicked letters, and, at the same time, were publicly absolving the queen.

In England, Elizabeth was assured that Mary was forced to be Bothwell's wife, and that he kept his former wife in his house, and would not have allowed Mary to live with him for half a year. Yet, Mary was so infatuated that she surrendered and offered to give up her realm. Sir Nicholas Throckmorton, the English envoy, spoke about Mary "with respect and reverence. . ." Lethington, as her friend, declared to Throckmorton that the preachers, the populace, and the chief nobles wished to take Mary's life. His bargain was "If Elizabeth interferes, Mary dies, and Elizabeth loses the Scottish Alliance."[39]

The Queen of Scotland was led to Edinburgh, then to the inland dungeon of Lock Leven where she was under lock and key. Her jewels included the ruby tortoise given by Riccio, the enamel of the mouse and the ensnared lioness, to be given to Lethington as a token. The diamonds had been left to Mary by a name she did not mention. The red enamelled wedding ring was the gift of Darnley. The diamond worn in her bosom was the betrothal present of Norfolk. All these, and the donors also, were to die with her. Mary verbally offered, by Robert Melville to the lords, to make Murray the Regent. By name she commended all the heady, reliant men of her country, even her enemies. Those appointees included on the Council of Regency were Chatelherault, Huntly, Argyll, Atholl, Lennox, and Morton, Murray, Mar, and Glencairn. Mary would not abandon Bothwell.[40]

The lords coerced Mary with letters unknown to the public. On 21 July 1567, the English envoy Throckmorton visited her in prison. She was prevailed upon to sign an act of abdication of the throne of Scotland in favor of her son by Lord Darnley. If the Queen would not abdicate, they would charge her with incontinence with Bothwell and others, and the handwritten proof of the murder of her husband. The nobles extorted her assent. Already, Mary had made up her mind. While she was a captive, her signature was legally invalid, so she signed deeds of abdication, regency, and permission to crown her son. Abandoning Bothwell, Mary Stuart abdicated the throne of Scotland in favor of her infant son. Five days afterwards, on 25 July 1567, James VI of Scotland was crowned at Stirling Castle. However, Murray, Lennox, and Morton successively held the regency of the kingdom for over a decade. Throckmorton believed he had saved Mary's life, and his accomplice, Melville, plainly told Elizabeth so, and she recognized Mary's magic, beguiling words.[41]

Mary escaped from her island-prison at Loch Leven on 2 May 1568, a year after her marriage to her third husband, Bothwell. In a few days, joined by Argyll, who was attached to the Reformation, she found herself at the head of an army of 6000 men. Among them were fifes and drums corps. In hope of victory, she exposed herself to all perils. On the 12th of May, her army was defeated by the Regent Murray at Langside, near Glasgow. Four days afterwards, in spite of the entreaties of her best friends, Mary crossed the Solway Firth to England. She threw herself on the protection of Elizabeth, only to find herself the focus of Catholic opposition to Elizabeth, and a prisoner for life.[42]

Between 1562-1573 there was fighting between the Queen's Men and the King's Men. Mary's lawyer was not with her. The Lyon Herald, Patrick Hepburn, was burned in a plot to kill Murray before moving on to Sterling and to Edinburgh. And, Mary Fleming was holding Dumbarton Castle for the former queen.

The lords with letters to justify them, were in a relatively secure position. Later, these letters were presented to Elizabeth's Commission at Westminster. Both France and England were anxious to secure the person of the baby Prince James, and they had the alliance of Scotland to bestow the crown. Elizabeth was anxious to have the alliance of Scotland and to help a sister queen.[43]

Just after Mary's flight into England, her jailer at Carlisle stated that with Mary Seton, her attendant, the Queen had "the finest brusher of a woman's hair to be seen in any country. Yesterday and this day she did set such a curled hair upon the

Chapter 4: Mary Queen of Scots

Queen, that was said to be a periwig, that showed very delicately, and every other day she hath a new design of head dressing that setteth forth a woman gaily well." This time the reason was that Mary had her head shaved, probably for the purposes of disguise, according to her secretary Nau. Mary was flying from the fear of the fiery death at the stake, the punishment of husband-murder. Then her nerve broke down. She prayed for her life.[44]

To Cecil, Sir Francis Knollys said, "This lady and Princess is a notable woman. She showeth a disposition to speak much, to be bold, to be pleasant, and to be very familiar. She showeth a great desire to be avenged of her enemies, she showeth a readiness to expose herself to all perils in hope of a victory, she delighteth much to hear of hardiness and valiance, commending by name all approved hardy men of her country, although they be her enemies, and (she) concealeth no cowardice even in her friends."[45]

On 15 December 1568, in a "signed" letter to Parliament in Edinburgh, "She demanded permission to be heard in person or by deputy. ..to answer the false calumnies. . ." Again, Mary offered to lay down her crown and to submit to the laws she desired to be enforced against Darnley's murderers. If not heard, she protested all proceedings of Parliament. She made the same demand to be heard at Westminster in December 1568, but was not allowed to appear and defend herself. Some of her supporters felt James, at Stirling Castle, could never be king as long as his mother lived.

Complicated negotiations preceded the meeting of Elizabeth's Commissioners at York, in October 1568. The Casket Letters discovered in a silver "box," the size of a small trunk, in December 1568, were placed before those who examined Mary's case. The French texts were in accordance with the Scotch texts, and displayed. However, they were not shown to Elizabeth.[46]

On 30 June 1578 the first cousin of Darnley, Esmé Stewart, Seigneur d' Aubigny, arrived from France. Darnley's younger brother, Charles, Earl of Lennox had died, and left property to Esmé, now Earl of Lennox, who had interest in the royal succession, as did Arabella Stewart. Esmé Stewart made friends with adolescent King James, and became his advisor. He was created Duke of Lennox and influenced the king. Then, Esmé returned to France where he died in 1583. And, Ludowick Stewart became second Duke of Lennox.[47]

Plots followed. Mary was suspected of having been implemented in numerous plots. Secretary Cecil and ambassador Throckmorton were against Lethington coming to England. Mary constantly asked leave to appear in Westminster Hall, where she would be backed by her own voice and tears. She trusted a theatrical denial, according to some, but others conceived she had a better policy, that of blackmailing Lethington concerning Darnley's murder. Mary complained to Elizabeth that Lady Lennox was hounding Lennox to prosecute Mary. In French Sonnets Mary wrote of her loss of her dowry in France and her title as heir apparent of the crown of the realm of England. Mary hoped for her own restoration to the throne, and she wished to be placed on the throne of Elizabeth.[48]

The most famous plot was that of Antony Babington, born of an old Catholic family at Dethick, Derbyshire, England. He served for a short time as page to Mary when she was a prisoner at Sheffield. In 1586, he was persuaded to head a conspiracy for Elizabeth's murder and Mary's release. Babington reserved the deliverance of Mary for his own share. He entered into correspondence with her, and received from her letters approving of the assassination. The plot was betrayed, and after hiding in St. John's Wood and at Harrow he was taken, and with thirteen others, he was executed in London on 20 September 1586.[49]

After this conspiracy was discovered, Mary was brought to trial. The sentence of death was pronounced against Mary on 15 October 1586. Seven days later, Mary consented to a London Conference, and expected a compromise. She would resign the crown and live affluently in England, and Murray would exercise the Regency. Mary's guilt could not be judicially proved. Murray was admitted to Elizabeth's presence at Hampton Court on 30 October 1586. Later, Mary was removed from Bolton, in the Manchester-Liverpool area, to Tutbury.[50]

Mary was five days' distance from her representatives. The winter weather was dreadful, the roads were foul, and communications were slow. She was not allowed to appear in her own defense, and this was disgraceful. Mary demanded to be heard in person before Elizabeth, the Peers, and the Ambassadors. However, in

Chapter 4: Mary Queen of Scots 55

December, when these demands were presented in person to Elizabeth by the Bishop of Ross, Mary was absent. Some of the Casket Papers produced were said to be copied from the French. "The Book of Articles" was read. There was much unscientific handling of these important documents. "No more preposterous proceedings were ever heard of in history."[51]

Mary, with her friends and foes, perverted the facts concerning Darnley's murder. On 1 February 1587, Elizabeth took the necessary courage to sign the warrant of execution. The blundering Scottish commissioners had no confidence in their cases. Mary's letters in French were possibly counterfeited, or forged, by secretary Lethington, and other voluminous material were discovered in her silver casket in a green cloth in June-July 1567.

The former Queen of Scots, "heard the English service with a book of psalms in English in her hand."[52] On the charges of sedition against her, Mary was beheaded on the scaffold at Fotheringhay on 8 February 1587. When her feet went down and her lips dropped, her end was bitter and sharp as a two-edged sword. Her blundering commissioners had none of her courage, and Elizabeth was unwilling to make arrangements for Mary to be heard. When these puzzling plots and notes were discovered, they were pondered by the world. Despite Mary's struggle for survival, she never tried to defend herself. She never met Elizabeth. She accepted her fate. The Privy Council of Queen Elizabeth I of England took the responsibility for Mary's execution.[53]

After Elizabeth's death, Mary's son, James VI, ruled England in peace. This king, a student of Calvin's theology, sanctioned the voyages of many Protestants who quietly left Ports in England to settle at Jamestown, Virginia.

Chapter 5
MARY DUDLEY SIDNEY, Countess of Pembroke
(1531 - 1586)

Mary, eldest daughter of Admiral John Dudley, Duke of Northumberland, and Anne Guildford, made personal sacrifices to promote thoughts of peace among colonists in the New World. Mary traveled with her husband Sir Henry Sidney to royal courts in England, Spain, France, Wales, and Ireland. She shared her goodwill in conversations with kings and queens, and with fishermen. During complicated times and discouraging circumstances in the mid-sixteenth century, Mary Sidney, Countess of Pembroke, generously contributed to financing discoveries in the New World.[1]

Professor John Dee was employed by Admiral Dudley and his wife to educate Mary and her brothers about the geography of the New World. This Protestant mathematician instructed Mary and her five brothers John, Ambrose, Guildford, Robert, and Henry about rivers and mines and trading posts for wool. On the map of South America, Dr. Dee pointed his wand to recently discovered Montevideo on the La Plata River and to territories where gold ore existed. By rounding the dangerous whirlpools in the Strait of Magellan, he foresaw that metals could be discovered in the Andes Mountains in Peru. Dr. Dee encouraged Mary to make appropriate notes on her slate about gold and wool, and to include descriptions of imports from abroad in permanent records in *My Ladies' Book*. These geography lessons about trading posts and prospective gold mines stimulated Mary to adore the teacher and support his objectives abroad.[2]

When the coronation procession of Edward VI left the Tower of London in 1547, sixteen-year-old Mary was attracted to the king's chamberlain, Sir Henry Sidney. While observing him ride ahead of fifty soldiers on horses, Mary admired his pleasant disposition and putty colored complexion. Sidney, knighted in 1550, discussed in her presence his interest in science and naval matters in America and Cathay. Between 1547 and 1553, Mary and Henry laughed on the river bank at a wiggly worm that dangled on the fishing line. The engaged couple studied plans for settlements in the New World.

Henry confessed the reasons for his fondness for his constant companion, frail King Edward VI, "As he grew in years and discretion, so grew I in liking of him."[3] When the young king died in the chamberlain's arms in 1553, his friend's name was attached to King Edward's will. This bequeathed to Henry Sidney the royal grant of the manor Skybeck, in Kent, in the commandery of the Knights of St. John of Jerusalem. The gift indicated Henry and the King had been interested in helping others.

In the sixteenth century, kings and queens contributed to this international institution known as the Hospitallers of St. John of Jerusalem, a military order founded to care for the poor and strangers in the Holy Land. Henry Sidney's ancestors were on the roster of the Knights of Rhodes, later known as Knights in Malta in the cathedral at Valetta. The crusaders in the society fought against the Moors, Arabs and Jews. On these Mediterranean islands dominated by the French and their heirs, the Knights, Chaplains and Serving Brothers of Arms were united. These crusaders had functioned with the spirit of christianity under eight "langues" of the commandery on the island of Rhodes, and then under the Maltese Cross. They operated charitable hospitals in Navarre, France, Italy, Ireland, Germany, Scotland, Castile, Crato, and Portugal. Good Knights were Masters of the Hospices, and the English connections were operated by charitably oriented priests. The English priories included Skybeck and Cranborne, in Kent, and Buckland and Sutton-at-Home in Devonshire. For the Knights of St. John, Henry kept meticulous records about the iron mines at Skybeck. At his elbow, Mary attempted to interpret the 'langues' of the countries and discussed potential settlements of the crusaders of

Chapter 5: Mary Dudley Sidney

the Order of St. John.[4]

While ambassador Sidney was on a diplomatic mission to Spain, his betrothed informed him about northern and southern discoveries made by Devonshire fishermen in the New World. The Sidneys also supported Sebastian Cabot, explorer and cartographer from Spain.[5]

The couple approved the plan to strengthen England's lagging economy and the Cathay Company. Englishmen willing to colonize America included Sir Francis Russell, Lord William Howard, Sir William Cecil, Sir Edward Horsey, Sir Henry Grey, Lord De la Warr, George and William Winter.[6] Approximately 200 merchants were seriously interested in extending the wool trade and acquiring gold mines in Peru. Several thousand adventurers in small ships were readied to sail down the Amazon River and overtake unsuspecting Spanish colonies in South America.

On 8 May 1553, the public wedding of Mary Dudley to Sir Henry Sidney was solemnized in Ely Palace, Holburn, near London.[7] After the ceremony, the bride learned to cope with fifty gentlemen and yeomen wearing badges indicating connections with the great plan to conquer the New World. While Henry was an ambassador from England to courts in France and Spain, Mary managed retainers over and above the menial servants at her home.

After the death of Edward VI, Mary dreaded her involvement in the awesome plot of placing Jane Grey on the throne of England. Following the wedding of Mary's brother Guildford to Jane in 1553, Henry Sidney rode with rioters in Northumberland's army. Mary assumed the peaceful duties of a lady-in-waiting on the privy council of her sister-in-law Queen Jane. She attended the "nine-day-queen" when Jane sailed from Greenwich castle up the Thames for the official crowning ceremony in the Tower of London. When the royal ship docked at the wharf, Mary escorted the newly crowned queen of England into the royal apartments, and attended Her Majesty.

After Lady Jane Grey's capture, Mary's brother, Robert Dudley, was imprisoned in the Tower and scheduled to die because he also aided in the wedding of Jane to Guildford. When led to the Guildhall, Mary listened to legal procedures concerning this queen's abortive reign. Weeks later, from the window in the house of Partridge, she and Jane watched Guildford go forth from Beauchamp Tower to his execution on Tower Hill, and they saw his headless body brought to the Chapel "in a carre."

Mary heard the hammering on the scaffold in preparation for Jane's execution on 12 February 1554. Terrified and mentally unable to cope with the situation, this lady-in-waiting courageously separated herself from the ex-queen and her attendants.[8]

Mary fled from the Tower of London to avoid arrest and death, and joined her husband on a voyage to France and Spain. Upon arrival in Spain, the Sidneys repeated news about dreadful acts that took place on the scaffold on Tower Hill. Her father, the duke of Northumberland, was executed in 1553, and her brother, Guildford, was beheaded on the chopping block in 1554. Her sister-in-law Jane suffered a private execution on Tower Green on 12 February 1554. And, the ex-queen's father, Sir Henry Grey, Duke of Suffolk, was later executed. Mary's mother, Catherine, the daughter of Charles Brandon, first Duke of Suffolk, also had fled overseas incognito.

While Mary feared for her life and that of her unborn child, she generated goodwill and peace in the court of King Philip of Spain. Although a refugee, she retained her position in England under the newly crowned Queen Mary, daughter of Catherine of Aragon. Henry was ideally suited to promote the wedding of Queen Mary to Philip of Spain, scheduled to take place in April 1554.

In a confidential letter from Spain to Her Majesty in England, Mary stated, "I am pregnant, afraid to travel, (and) hesitate to return to England with my offspring."[9]

The Sidney's oldest child, born 30 November 1554 in Spain, was christened "Philip," in honor of King Philip of Spain. On this occasion, King Philip of Spain stood as godfather to the infant Philip Sidney, to show the English ambassador and his charming wife the greatest honor. Philip was a special person.[10]

When appointed an ambassador to Paris in 1556, Henry and his wife showed the French Court their understanding about the New World settlements. They were

Chapter 5: Mary Dudley Sidney

so well received by Admiral Coligny and Jeanne d'Albret, Queen of Navarre, that the Sidneys became part of the French colonization projects to America.

After Mary Tudor died in November 1558, and Queen Elizabeth I ascended the English throne, the Sidneys returned to England. They opened doors of Penshurst estate, in Kent, to students and neighbors. Henry assumed the financial obligations of the faculty pensioners of non-functioning Tattersall College in Lincolnshire. And, Mary had inherited the manors of her father.[11]

Mary acted as hostess, confidant, and counselor to inquiries about her sister-in-law Amy Robsart who had married Mary's brother Robert on 4 June 1550 in the royal palace of Sheen, Surrey. In order to achieve financial security Sir John Dudley and Sir John Robsart had arranged this union, and they exchanged several manors. Amy's chief source of income was money derived from the sale of wool, and she led a simple country life. For entertainment she worked with servants, sang ballads, and visited fairs. During these years of marriage, Amy felt neglected because Robert was notoriously friendly with Queen Elizabeth. And, while he attended Mary of Guise in Scotland, he experienced the lighthearted ways of the French court.[12]

Robert, condemned to death in 1554, remained in prison until he was pardoned. In the first year of Queen Elizabeth's reign, Robert was promoted to positions connected with Her Majesty. While riding on royal hunts in stylish clothes, he became Master of the Horse, and was chosen a Knight of the Garter. He encouraged Her Majesty to slit the throats of captured deer. He sent skinned otters, pregnant pigs, and boar to Amy to prepare for dinner parties. Robert, the keeper of run-down Kenilworth Castle, was in charge of hunting, tilting, and military games. The pleasures he planned for Elizabeth's ladies and knights included dancing, plays, contests, and pageants.

While Amy resided at Cumnor Hall, Berkshire, she was nervous and convinced of her husband's hatred, and some thought he might marry Queen Elizabeth if he was free. When Amy fell headlong down a dangerous staircase and broke her neck, this was apparently accidental.

At Amy's funeral at Oxford in 1559, Mary heard the chaplain remark, "This poor lady . . .so pitifully murdered."

Courtiers at a water party at Greenwich on 3 November 1559, whispered about this charge of "foul play." They asked Mary, "Why was no inquiry made? Why did Robert fail to appear? Why did he remain silent?" The suspicion about Robert's affair with the Queen placed additional stress upon Mary to answer questions about her brother's wife.[13]

In 1564, Robert Dudley, notorious on the Privy Council, was created Earl of Leicester by Queen Elizabeth. Later, he wore elegant armor embossed with his badge of a bear and ragged staff. When the Leicester Buildings were renovated for more stylish living, Mary, wary of the queen's ideas, wondered why Robert became the great builder of Kenilworth.[14]

Mary duplicated methods her parents used to achieve Philip's interest in the New World. The Sidneys' children Mary, Margaret, Elizabeth, Robert and Thomas arrived in quick succession. Then, in similar arrangements, Dr. John Dee returned to Penshurst at nominal expense to teach her son Philip and her other children math and naval matters. Neighbors and friends were also invited to Penshurst to learn about these subjects. The professor accepted an invitation to Queen Elizabeth's privy chamber, where he explained to Her ladies possibilities in the New World. At Penshurst, Dr. Dee's presentations some families such as De la Warr and Darracott were included because of connections with the Order of the Knights of St. John. Dr. Dee also discussed with Westcountrymen and with Oxford University and Middle Temple students, including barrister John Dodderidge, connected with Sutton-at-Home. Imminent plans plans of northeastward and northwestward voyages to Cathay were presented to men interested in colonization. Adventurers Humphrey Gilbert, Walter Raleigh, John Davis, Richard Grenville and George Clifford were among those inspired to set sail to lands beyond the sea and to Cathay. The expedition of John Davis to Mt. Sidney, Newfoundland, in search of a passage to China, was supported by others. The Sidneys also contributed to two voyages to Florida, and they sponsored Grenville's voyages to Roanoke Island.[15]

Due to the Sidneys' efforts, Penshurst gained the reputation for scholarship, and became a center for young men to study the geography of the New World.

Chapter 5: Mary Dudley Sidney

Among the daily facts Mary recorded in *My Ladies Book* were references to a pleated crimson taffeta bed cover. Rarely idle, she regularly kept accurate household accounts, recorded stipends, and signed five pound, weekly receipts. She gingerly spent one pound of allowance to play with Henry at the gaming tables. According to *My Ladies Book*, she ordered bells and string to amuse Henry's pet monkey.[16]

On evenings at Penshurst, an Italian servant helped her into fashionable velvet dresses, and fastened an expensive gold chain about her stately neck. Musicians played on virginals and stringed instruments. This lady ate from her own silver plate, enjoyed wine from her silver tankard, and sipped from her personal cup. She planned hawking, hunting and swimming parties to other manors. When Henry relaxed, he read aloud from three books of *Martyrs* and looked through pictures in Froissart's *Chronicles*.[17] The stimulating life at Penshurst was arranged according to the demands of Mary's children, husband, and the Queen.

Notes in *My Ladies Book* divulged that Mary relaxed at several English manors in England, and decided to be of service in Ireland. The devastating scorched earth policy of burning crops in Ulster, Ireland, caused soldier Henry to kiss his wife and their son Philip "goodbye." Because the Sidneys had enthusiastically supported the newly crowned Queen of England, Henry was sworn in as Chief Justice of Ireland.

When Henry directed fierce fighting as Lord Lieutenant of Ireland in 1565, Mary received his flattering letter, asking her to come live with him during the war. By rights, a woman of this era was allowed to follow her husband into the battlefield if she wished. Mary responded, "What can be more glorious than to be of service to our country?"[18]

Ireland to Penshurst, and to court to attend the Queen, became Mary's itinerary. She rarely complained while traveling in the wagon covered with hides and trimmed with silk from Germany. A Dutch wagoner was employed for these bumpy journeys back and forth over the exhausting route to a castle, and to Dublin, Her Majesty's chief city in Ireland. Although Mary survived voyages over the wild Irish sea, this stressful life took its toll on her health. Her doctor prescribed almonds, asparagus, bark of lignin, and sarsaparilla, and also ordered a cordial diluted with goat's milk and ginger to encourage rest.[19] These travels recorded in her diary survived for centuries. According to *The Image of Ireland*, written by a close observer, chaos and anarchy prevailed on the island.

Mary met enemies to peace, disturbers of the commonwealth, and she realized why they were considered monsters. She showed goodwill to the famous archer Rorie Rogue, called Rone Oge when he submitted peacefully to Henry in Ireland. She was exposed to the habits and apparel of Woodkarne, and to their aptness to rebel against the queen. In their nakedness, they cast their eyes down to the ground, damning, condemning. Along the flowing streams and rivers, famous for fish, were cattle and wild fowl on the land, that gave pleasure to men. In the shaking bog, generations of Irish nymphs had pleasurable pastimes such as retaining wolves and cherishing serpents. According to *The Image of Ireland,* Henry was likened to King Arthur by showing his magnanimity in right things including wisdom, knowledge, and judgment. He abolished fear, and was inspired to give peace to the worthy in Ireland.[20]

Whenever possible, Henry wrote their son Philip about rules of conduct of life. In one letter Philip was urged to pray at an ordinary hour, to study diligently, and to "mark the matter of that which you read" . . . "to be humble to your master" . . . "courteous, moderate in diet and drink". . . "to exercise your body, to be clean." His advice was to "be merry, but without biting words to any man, to tell no untruth. You descend from noble blood on your mother's side, and must be an ornament to our illustrious family."[21]

On 16 June 1578, Dublin was torn by religious differences, and Mary depended upon God's direction to show her the best place to live inexpensively. For her children's sake, she preferred to fund the war in Ireland and to live at home. Upon returning to Penshurst with Henry, she pled poverty and asked Queen Elizabeth for some slight assistance. She hoped Henry, who sacrificed health and pleasure for the crown, would be made a Baron and have additional revenue for the family. Because Henry loved good society and hospitality, Mary entertained lavishly at banquets, and purchased appealing presents for the queen. Occasionally, she acquired a new velvet gown and silk hose and financed these at her expense.[22]

As a lady-in-waiting, Mary became a day and night nurse, and she sacrificed herself personally for ailing Queen Elizabeth. Hourly, she sponged Her Majesty's burning body covered with small pox, and she even probed into terrifying, festering sores. Cheerfully, she wiped the queen's drooling mouth, and nursed and mothered her back to life. Hardly a blemish remained on the queen's face because of Mary's interest. While England gloried in Elizabeth's miraculous recovery, something frightening about Mary's once beautiful features reflected in the hand mirror. When Mary contracted the small pox, she proved she loved England more than herself. Knowingly, she had sacrificed her beauty and health for the sake of the queen. However, Mary received no commendation or compensation from Her Majesty. Ignoring the horrible, permanent holes in his wife's cheeks, forehead, and nose, long-suffering Henry drew her close and professed his love for his unselfish wife.[23]

The queen, typical of a self-serving ruler seeking power and lacking appreciation, was spoiled and critical of this lady-in-waiting. Elizabeth seldom properly welcomed the Sidneys in keeping with their public service to England and the British Isles. The childish queen barely acknowledged the costly gold jewel presented her by Henry on New Year's Day. When this sacrificial gift was ignored, tears streamed down Mary's deeply pocked cheeks.[24] Shortly afterwards, Sir Henry Sidney was appointed the Lord President of the Council of Wales to illustrate he was one of Her Majesty's favorites. Mary realized Henry must be a favorite ruler of the English queen because they occupied Ludlow Castle, Shropshire, on a cliff overlooking the River Teme in Wales. This ideal site for a fortress had a beautiful Norman chapel on the strategic Welsh borders. The extensive gatehouse on the north side was an architectural improvement. In the Great Hall, Mary listened to Henry read aloud about the history of shepherds and water nymphs in Wales. In 1581, he declared, "a better people to govern than the Welsh, Europe holdeth not."[25]

When the Sidneys returned to Penshurst, Henry spent much time with Mary at court, and declared he loved her with all his heart, mind and soul. She shed tears of happiness when he held her close to vow, "You are a full, fair lady."[26]

Mary again was forced to travel from Penshurst by land and sea to Flushing,

Ireland, because Henry lay stricken with arthritis, diseases, and painful stones in his bladder. According to the physician's remedial exercises, stones were tied around his ankles and he was encouraged to raise one foot at a time, to try to walk without limping, but each step was agony. He worried over family finances and field atrocities. In 1586, in the bishop's palace at Worcester Sir Henry died prematurely, in his fifties. His heart was buried at Ludlow, Wales. However, the queen ordered his body embalmed and sent to Penshurst with great solemnity.[27]

In her declining years, Mary encouraged her son Sir Philip Sidney, now Governor of Flushing, Ireland, with his plans for a perfect existence in a wonderful country. In 1578, he was known as Knight of the Most Noble Order of the Garter, and Lord Deputy General of her highness' realm in Ireland. In 1582, his mother read Philip's name and the inscription of his college friend Richard Hakluyt in the first collection of *Voyages*. Mary noticed Philip's habit of turning his eyes westward.

When Philip served in Parliament in 1579, he entertained high officials without regard to race or color. At the beginning of 1583, Philip had been attentive to Queen Elizabeth. He presented Her Majesty with a golden flowerpot, and he received the gracious gift of a lock of the royal virgin's hair. He even obtained the honor of knighthood, and divulged his plans to write about Utopia.

Some courtiers considered Philip's ideals of a Utopia an impracticable goal. He planned life on an imaginary island similar to the one described by Sir Thomas More in 1516 as a seat of perfection in moral, social and political line. In this social theory, he preferred the simple, rural life of poets. Philip planned a Utopia where everyone would live without persecution and would witness mock alliances, laughter, truces and crimes of violence.

Included in his plan for a Utopia were Don Antonio, King of Portugal, the King of Navarre, and the Kings of Poland, Sweden, Barbary and Morocco. Obviously, Philip was acquainted with Don Antonio, King of Portugal, when he was in Devonshire. Philip was familiar with the camels in Morocco, and the slaves in Barbary, and he secured the crown's support in Poland and Sweden. By lending financial support, Mary also approved her son's ambitious project of a Utopia at

Chapter 5: Mary Dudley Sidney 67

Providence Island, Panama, for free trade for friendly merchants overseas. Specific nations would trade with inhabited plantations chosen by benefactors. English merchandise would be accepted, and Spanish enterprises omitted.

When he was young, Philip, at little additional cost, had attended Henry on a diplomatic assignment in France. The youth was indoctrinated with ideals of chivalry known only in secret religious orders such as the Knights of Malta. At Pau Castle, Navarre, Philip met popular Prince Henry, the son of Jeanne d'Albert, Queen of Navarre, who later became King Henry IV of France. This country in southern France, formerly considered a part of Spain, had dangerous precipices and glaciers. Mary's favorite son drank of the water of the hot springs. He fenced, vaulted, wrestled, and cast stones. He fished and jumped rocks, tamed bears, and captured squirrel. On the streets of Auch, Prince Henry rode a superb Andalusian horse, black as jet, branded "H.N." From the balcony of Penshurst, Philip reported these experiences in southern France and the Greek islands to various gatherings.

Philip's poetical ideas about a mountainous area in Peloponnesus, Greece, were presented as a Utopia. He promoted a municipal government resembling a small Greek republic that could have equal distribution of property. The richest men raised horses for the cavalry, and the chevaliers owned horses, while the foot-captains, the squires, and the nobles were without fortune. In a "lay abbey," the baron collected tithes, and possessed the right of patronage. There would be free trade and divine right in the simple, rustic settlement of common men. Every man could have as much land as he could work in one day. Military service would be restricted and commercial liberty with free trade would result. There would be the payment of a single tax. Family feasts would be conspicuous because of wine and delicious food, as described by poets in *Arcadia*. This would be a simple, pastoral settlement.[28] In one charter from the crown, projects for colonization, or plantation, were already afloat among West country gentlemen Sir Humphrey Gilbert, Walter Raleigh, and Sir George Peckham, and others.[29] The charter colony was to settle on an island towards the west.

Queen Elizabeth gave a second charter of lands to Sir Henry Sidney -- a pretty little estate of three millions of acres in North America. And, he was granted land on the Chesapeake Bay known as "Brandon," the name of his grandmother.[30]

Mary heard, "He won thirty gentlemen of great blood and state. . . every man to sell one hundred pounds land for fitting out a fleet." Philip was to go alone to Plymouth. This plan necessitated transporting negroes and supplies, and meeting Francis Drake at Plymouth to depart. She believed Philip would become a governor in the New World.[31]

Mary was stunned to learn of the Queen's preplanned plots whereby Queen Elizabeth had ordered Philip to the Lowland skirmishes. Some said Her Majesty believed Philip would be safer with his Uncle Robert. Furthermore, Drake had played Philip false, deserted him, and sailed southward without him.[32] His mother could not be comforted.

Nor could she reconcile herself to the terrible blow of his death in 1586. Ironically, Philip Sidney, named in honor of Philip of Spain, had died in a war against Spain, while serving under his uncle Leicester. His splendid and costly funeral at Penshurst was well attended by knights carrying banners of chivalry.[33]

Mary sought comfort under the sturdy Penshurst oaks. She remembered Philip's career was hampered by relationship to her brother Robert, Earl of Leicester. Talking to the mirror, she recalled Henry's efforts to establish good government in Ireland and in England. She believed Philip was the most able of many men who ruled Ireland under Elizabeth.

Mary turned her thoughts to her marriage to Henry. She pictured Henry as an excellent speaker, and praised him. The historian in *Image of Ireland* stated, "Though unrewarded by the sovereign to whose service he devoted his life, his death was bitterly bemoaned by all those who had the interests of good government at heart, and posterity has done him ample justice."[34]

Because their marriage was one of exceptional communion between man and woman, Mary did not survive Henry long. Within a few months, she was laid by his side in Penshurst Church on 11 August 1586.[35] Mary Sidney's unselfish patriotism and reputation of goodwill as Henry's wife and Philip's mother lived on in the New World.

Chapter 6
MADEMOISELLE HORSEY
(c1535 - ante 1583)

Mademoiselle, born and bred in the powerful state of Normandy, became the bride of soldier Edward Horsey. As the first Lady Governor of the Isle of Wight, she assumed responsibilities beyond her wifely duties. During the religious wars, Mademoiselle preferred her Normandy background remain anonymous, although she deserved recognition for tributes to the Protestant clique. Her taste for adventure enabled her to save the lives of her husband's group. Furthermore, she ministered to the needs of those adhering to the Reformation.

Mademoiselle inherited the knowledge of how to entertain nobility, and she cheerfully responded to natives. She deplored the charges written in Latin in diplomatic meetings of the English government. And, she dealt with the disasters of France. Her main method of survival was to retain her maiden form of address, "Mademoiselle."

Cousins bred in Normandy inherited a spirit of independence, and participated with zest in women's activities, such as swinging arms and walking barefoot on the beach, and chanting like crusaders. They enjoyed sea-bathing on the jagged coastline.

In 1553 when they discovered soldier-sailors in a sinking ship, Mademoiselle and her cousin displayed the courage and nautical knowledge indigenous to their forebears. Reared with the laws and experiences afforded by the sea and God, the cousins with helping hands participated in dangerous rescues at sea. They had no qualms about the circumstances.[1]

Whenever possible, Mademoiselle traveled on voluntary pilgrimages to the Woman's Abbey at Caen. They heard about the unique late eleventh-century tapestry de Bayeux preserved in storage. According to womens' recollections, this measured 20 feet wide by 241 feet long. Six centuries after completion, the embroidered scenes of the Norman Conquest would hang in the huge Lisieux Cathedral and reveal the expression of soldier-sailors of fortune leaving the Norman shore in small ships. These scenes preserved in storage in the town of Bayeux, depicted the victory of William the Conqueror in England when his men triumphed over the heathen.[2]

On clear days, Mademoiselle climbed the steep uphill path to Mont Saint-Michel that was surrounded by water during high tides. The priory, where Benedictine monks lived in a mammoth house, included a hall, pantry, buttery, winery, and dairy. The kitchen was replete with pots, pans, and plates and wooden saucers. From the monks, Mademoiselle gleaned specific information from historic charts about paths of the sea. Facing westward, she traced the routes of Columbus and sailors crossing the Atlantic Ocean. Turning from this vantage point at the mountain peak, Mademoiselle identified flags on ships heading southward towards the Protestant ports Rochelle on the Gironde River, and St. Jean-de-Luz on the Bay of Biscay. Among these were Dutch, Huguenot, English, and Portuguese. Experienced with maritime affairs, on a clear day she sighted special moorings on a strip of land separated from England by a narrow channel on a green sea.

There were barges with Huguenot flags on the island of Guernsey. People of the Channel Islands of Guernsey, Jersey, and the Isle of Wight were interrelated, and experienced with maritime affairs. The area was fast becoming a haven for Protestant rovers. In 1553, at the beginning of the rule of Queen Mary in England, the time was ripe in Normandy to rebel against the Old Learning and join the Protestant cause. To avoid being cut off from the homeland by the rising tide, Mademoiselle and her cousin clasped hands and hastily descended the steep hill from Mont Saint-Michel. During harvest time in the wheat fields of Normandy, they helped old women wearing red bandannas. The girls dressed in dark, ankle length skirts and long sleeved blouses to harvest, cut, and tie bundles of grain. They heard the constant complaint, "Rich employers and tyrannical nobility harass us."[3]

The cousins practiced paddling a skiff loaded with wine on the Cher River. They glided through the graceful arches of Chenonceau, the jewel of all castles in the Loire River valley. They heard whispers about library drawers and secret lockers filled with poisons by evil Catherine d'Medici, the Queen Mother. At Chenonceau Castle the King's mistress Dianne de Poitiers had tended the vegetable and rose gardens with the high border of boxwood edging that she planted to hide prying eyes. Because Mademoiselle inherited a horticultural background, she memorized names of these herbs and vegetables suitable for her future use in a garden at home.[4]

Cousins in red boots sailed in a three-masted schooner to Chambord Castle, and the hunting reserve. At this destination, protesting servants hauled firewood up numerous steps on the monumental staircase with two winding spirals that never met. On the landings were majestic porcelain stoves. From the third landing they could see a stone ceiling decorated with the salamander. From the terrace, visitors strolled among the chimneys, the turrets, and bell towers to the chapel. And, they admired a huge lantern decorated with a fleur-de-lys on the grand staircase.

Atop the fourth landing, Mademoiselle viewed the thick forest of trees in the palace park, where banquets, masquerades, and fireworks took place. She remembered the deer, doe, wild boar, and foxes. Her cousins pointed to pheasants, ducks, and wild cats in the Norway pines. Rebellious Huguenots described these entertainments that prolonged their visit as "all hallmarks of a corrupt society."

Despite the permanent red stains on their wearing apparel, girls in their teens unloaded casks of red wine to the Dinard wharf. Here, they acquired permanently stained hands, feet, toes, and clothes. The lush bunches of red grapes had been squeezed, pushed and pressed under beams on a turn-around wheel in a dark, musty cave near Bordeaux. Treasonable conversations were repeated verbatim. At the waterside, port authorities blamed wealthy barons for the deplorable working conditions. The wines transported by mule-back to Dinard were shipped via Devonshire to the English court.

On a historic day in 1553 on the foggy Normandy beachhead, Mademoiselle and her favorite cousin reminisced about dangerous weather and rip tides in the English Channel. Suddenly, they spotted a Huguenot flag on a crowded flyboat pitching about in roaring surf. They heard shouts of terror from soldiers attempting an unexpected landing. The ancient herring boat, with a broken rudder and splintered hull, breached and floundered. The lead-line failed to indicate a safe landing spot, and suggestions of Mademoiselle were lost in the wind.

These cousins caught, with nautical expertise, the bow line thrown with force from the sinking ship. After Commander Edward Horsey, his brother Francis, and soldiers reached safe footing ashore, the rescuers and the crew dropped to their knees to praise God. Obviously, these Englishmen on a secret Protestant mission were fearful of capture. This was probably the reason why Edward and his brother, Francis Horsey, of a well-known Devonshire family, followed the girl guides to a lonely area.

Commander Horsey implied the soldiers-sailors were hunted by English authorities. They could be implicated as pirates, and considered outlaws from justice. The Horsey brothers belonged to a Protestant conspiracy that included Ambassador Nicholas Throckmorton and merchants associated with the New Learning clique. The commander sought funds to help Huguenot refugees change the power of monarchs. And, his crew sought help from the French nobility in the popular plan to dethrone Queen Mary in England, in favor of Princess Elizabeth.

The real heroines credited with saving the lives of the Horsey crew were Mademoiselle and her cousin.[5] The nautical young women were familiar with friendly ports on the Channel Islands where war supplies and furnishings were donated to the New Learning of Protestants.

Supporters of the Channel Island project included Robert, son of Admiral John Dudley, and survivors of this family, such as Sir Henry Sidney and Sir Francis Russell, and also Sir William Cecil. High-ranking Naval Board friends were Admiral William Winter and his brother George, from Barnstaple.[6] On the islands, these avid volunteers for the New Learning stocked shipping barges and fishing boats with maritime supplies.[7]

Chapter 6: Mademoiselle Horsey

When the Horsey brothers joined Mademoiselle and her cousin, they became a friendly foursome of the Protestant clique. The girls quickly secured a skiff, and the group sailed to a distant landing on a little-known island in the English Channel. Here, the couples took marriage vows in a secret wedding ceremony.

Commander Horsey used personal charm and halting French to indicate that his group of exiles sympathized with members of the New Learning clique. His twelve supportive associates had recently attempted to rob the English Exchequer of a fifty-thousand-pound deposit rightfully belonging to Protestant supporters of Jane Grey. Those apprehended were found guilty, and hanged as traitors. The survivors intended to operate from the Channel Islands to reclaim money belonging to the Protestant treasury. They were considered as half-pirates, half-soldiers from England.

Mademoiselle willingly dealt with the disasters of France and England. Her knowledge of French and the French ports enabled her husband to obtain small, efficient boats. She felt secure in her efforts when the Commander interpreted an English law, "If a man and woman committed a felony it is considered the husband's fault."[8]

Commander Horsey used Mademoiselle's expertise in French affairs to gain a midnight audience with the French King, Henry II. And, with the king, they made diplomatic arrangements for Princess Elizabeth to marry Sir Edward Courtenay, of the De Rivers family, currently confined in the Tower of London.[9]

And, Horsey's bride helped to solicit funds from the king for the Protestant uprising to place Princess Elizabeth upon the English throne. Her clique received a small amount of money and the tentative promise for more. In the end, the conference was of no avail. However, the commander received a commission from Admiral Coligny to operate a boat with a French flag.

In 1556, at night, the French bride of the commander further served the clique. She stealthily led Ambassador Throckmorton into a small unidentified room. The Protestant group gathered around a table, and she lit candles for the clandestine meeting of supporters of New Learning. A secret oath was taken on the Bible. One agreement enabled them to counterfeit sufficient English coins from

Spanish silver to pay forces to land refugees on the Channel Islands. These sparsely settled places were nameless islands including Guernsey, Jersey, and the Isle of Wight. The bride's assistance in this wild plot enabled Commander Horsey and others to become recognized as valuable to the cause of placing Princess Elizabeth on the throne of England.[10]

Furthermore, the newlyweds, Commander Horsey and his wife, offered assistance with personal contributions to transport Huguenots briefed in the New Learning to Rio de Janerio on the Amazon River, and to the land of gold. And, their group supported a second attempt to make a French settlement in South America.[11]

According to Robert Dudley, later created Earl of Leicester, gold to be sent to the pope was routinely hauled aboard to waiting Spanish vessels near Panama. It was deemed necessary for English ships to dominate the mining of Peruvian gold in order to gain sway over part of Brazil. The consensus of this group was that the English could safely navigate the Amazon, and climb and cross the Andes to Peru where gold and silver mines were abundant.[12]

Following the death of Queen Mary and the ascent of Protestant Princess Elizabeth to the English throne, French nobles were encouraged to help refugees in exile. A product of country living and member of the New Learning group, Madamoiselle Horsey assisted Protestant exiles to return to England. In 1559, the Channel Islands were easily conquered by the forces of Admiral Winter, of Devonshire. By 18 February 1562, Edward Horsey was knighted in England by Queen Elizabeth. And, he ingratiated himself with Robert Dudley, later Earl of Leicester.

In December 1565, Commander Horsey was nominated a commissioner of the Isle of Wight, a haven for religious cults where democracy could flourish. Edward speedily became Captain-Governor of this island. And, Mademoiselle from Normandy became the First Governor's Wife of the Isle of Wight.[13] The De Insula Family had owned the Isle of Wight. In the latter part of the twelfth century, Isabel de Rivers granted land to Robertus D'Arricau.[14] Jean Martin, Jean Delacourt, and Thomas West were among the self-perpetuating oligarchy of related commissioners. The island had become a democracy.[15]

Chapter 6: Mademoiselle Horsey

Edward and his wife joined the French group of people that included Jeanne, Queen of Navarre, Ambassador Henry Sidney, and Admiral Coligny. The New Learning constituents made preparations to transport a group consisting of a few noblemen and brave laborers, mostly Calvinists, to settle in America. Huguenot volunteers under Jean Ribault sailed in two staunch ships from Le Havre for America. Included in English sponsors were Jane Stuckley, the second daughter of Sir Lewis Pollard, Justice on the Queen's Bench. Seamen familiar with this region included navigator Rene de Laudonniere and Nicholas Barre, and soldiers.[16]

Avoiding the Spanish in the West Indies by taking a direct route across the Atlantic, Ribault reached America in April, in remarkable time. He proceeded northward along the Florida coast to the River of May, now the St. John's River. Ashore, the colonists knelt to give thanks to God. They prayed He would bless their enterprise, and that they would bring the knowledge of the Saviour to the heathen in the New World. Friendly natives gathered in a grove of cypress and palm trees, while Ribault set up a pillar of stone engraved with royal arms of France, indicating the formal possession of America for France.

Le Moyne's painting of Fort Caroline engraved by Theodore de Bry depicted a counterpart of a North Devon oven on a raised platform under a crude shed in 1564. In their sturdy ships, the French explored the coast northward to channel of Port Royal, and laid the foundations of the colony on Edisto Island, near Beaufort, South Carolina. The settlement was called Charles Fort in honor of the boy-king on the throne of France. Ribault and Laudonniere returned to report the discoveries to the King. However, many of the colony were eventually massacred. Only a few returned to France.

With the help of their relatives, Governor Horsey, Ambassador Henry Sidney, and nobleman Warham St. Leger supplied seven ships for a second group of New Learning settlers. This fleet carried nearly 1,000 soldiers, artisans and seamen, and the Protestant clergyman Robert. A third expedition sailed from Dieppe to cement their fortunes. However, because of their impressive voices, the psalm-singing crews were unpopular, and the fate of these Huguenots was to be dismembered, a disaster worse than death. And, Spaniards under Pedro Menendez de Abila claimed their territory for Spain.[17] The governor's wife on the Isle of Wight exuded charming hospitality during her husband's long absences. She welcomed disguised herring boats hoisting Huguenot flags, and she harbored sea rovers. The governor returned from the disastrous siege at Le Havre, where he had succeeded in having Calvin's brother-in-law, William Whittingham, made chaplain. And, the Governor declared to his wife that the Isle of Wight was his home.[18]

Recalling the herbs at Castle Chenonceau, the Governor's wife informed the natives of available remedies on ships returning to the Isle of Wight. She promoted the health products of natural foods and miracle cures designed to put a body in tune with nature. These included kina-kina seed, a useful cough remedy from Peru. The root of the valeriana plant served as a tranquilizer, and cocoa leaves chewed with a lime, brought relief from cocaine usage. The herbs planted under her direction, for cleansing and normalizing body functions, raised the energy level. And, as she thought God intended, she made available to Huguenot refugees the herbs that thrived on the Isle of Wight.

A vast New Forest of over 300 acres on the Isle of Wight was a crucial necessity for hungry refugees, as well as English and French sea rovers. In her endeavor to stock the wildlife preservation with game, the Governor's wife gave a lamb for every living hare brought to her home from neighboring counties. Animals multiplying quickly such as squirrels, deer, snakes, kingfishers, and partridges, found refuge in the New Forest.[19] And, among hundreds of waders off shore were many wildfowls and birds.

The position of this governor's wife was undefined. In preparation for the war against Spain, African animal skins were fashioned into leg protectors for soldiers. And, saltpeter for gunpowder was manufactured.[20] In 1569, at the outbreak of the northern rebellion, Governor Horsey was ordered to help the English. He was despatched at the head of five hundred well-furnished horsemen to help defeat the insurgents from the north. During the Governor's absences, his wife was in charge of the Isle of Wight. For seventeen years, she lived in perfect harmony with the black monks at Carysbrook Castle. As an official greeter, she welcomed French and English herring fishermen from the river, from the quays, and

Chapter 6: Mademoiselle Horsey

from the remote, clear water anchorage. With the courage of her Norman forefathers, and aided by her experience, she kept an expert lookout for foreign ships cruising the narrow seas. From the widow's walk atop the governor's mansion, she identified flags and detected pirates where salt pans and oyster beds thrived. In Newtown, a mile form Newport, his wife promoted peace with English and French people.

The interesting fact was that the first Governor's wife of the Isle of Wight, during his absences, acted in her husband's place for the English government. For Cecil, secretary to Queen Elizabeth, she kept a sharp lookout for alien ships in the English Channel, and reported those heavily laden of Spain. Fifty coffers of treasure were seized near her lookout position atop the Governor's mansion.[21]

However, according to English law a woman had no rights in parliament. Half-Norman and half-English, the feminine governor worried about her legal status and rights, and she felt like an alien.[22] Left alone to rule lawless islanders who distributed trash and garbage in streets and threw unsuspecting Frenchmen into the sea, she found it impossible to condone projects of theft, piracy, and counterfeiting coins for the sake of Protestantism.

As governor, Mademoiselle worked for France to overcome the wicked ways of corruption in French courts.[23] She entertained lavishly while Edward detained ships and men for an expedition in 1570. In her husband's absence, his wife was zealous in surveying the defenses of the Isle of Wight and ordering necessary repairs.[24] She furnished the governor's mansion on the Isle of Wight in keeping with the regal chateaux on the Loire. Her appointments in the governor's house included porcelain stoves, lavish tapestries, a marble staircase, like those at Chambord Castle and portraits of the governors of the Channel Islands. In addition, there were near-perfect table settings of gold and silver from a Huguenot sea rover.

This substitute governor strongly suspected piracy when she courageously dispatched ships to protect the island from the men-of-war cruising off shore, under the assumed authority of the Queen of Navarre. Vessels were instructed to watch the piratical craft hovering about the southern shores, and this lady directed their capture when necessary.

However, Governor Horsey and his substitute officer on the Isle of Wight were accused of complicity with their proceedings, and given a stern remonstrance from Cecil, secretary to Queen Elizabeth. This charge Horsey denied in 1570. The governor's wife acted as interpreter to idle young French nobles.

While Presbyterians planned a synodical meeting in 1572 on the island of Guernsey, she was accused by the justices in England of "complicity with piracy." In court, this lady claimed she could not comprehend the tedious charges of receiving presents of "sweetmeats, spices, and Canary wine," because the charges were written in Latin. She suggested everyone should be working for the Protestant cause, and she probably meant they should use English or French.[25]

Despite the facts that forty of her servants were down with the black plague and she had a sore throat, the governor's wife lavishly entertained the Portuguese ambassador. When he arrived with his entourage to visit in her household, she entertained him magnificently, with gaiety, and adroitly admired his jewels that had been stolen from an exiled monarch. She led the guests carrying glasses of wine from the library to the banquet hall buffet that was loaded with seasoned lamb, venison, rabbit and squirrel. She invited them to partake of homemade eclairs in the tapestry room where her husband described New World opportunities. At dinner, his brother, Sir Jerome Horsey, related his fascinating adventures on a recent trip to Russia.[26] Throughout these discussions and during his visit, the Portuguese ambassador never detected his hostess was operating a servantless household.[27]

The life of the governor's wife on the Isle of Wight was affected by French politics and by serious bloodshed. Among the difficult alliances was the marriage of Prince Henry, now King of Navarre and heir to the French throne, to Margaret of Valois. This marriage was witnessed by a hundred thousand Huguenots on 18 August 1572. By the union of the houses of Bourbon, Navarre and Valois, the bride's mother, Catherine d'Medici, hoped the wedding would guarantee peace between the two religions, Protestant and Catholic.[28]

Paris was alive with a spirit of hatred that affected the Huguenots and Catholic people. Ribbons of blue were strung in gay festoons from the windows. The royal guard included close friends and "gentlemen of the sword" with straight

Chapter 6: Mademoiselle Horsey

noses, grace, and penetrating eyes. In Paris, they took assumed names and used the fleur-de-lys. The daredevils used muskets to replace carbines on the saddle, and they wore gold lace cuffs under a great coat embroidered with silver crosses and jewels on black velvet. Part of their bountiful salary was used for good attire. Two by two on grey horses bedecked in ribbons, the King's Musketeers preceded others guards and accompanied the king everywhere. Their strength, courage, military spirit and discipline aroused envy.[29]

Prince Henry, son of Jeanne d'Albert, thought it unsuitable for him to be wedded to a Catholic, and he refused to be married under the rose window at Notre Dame Cathedral. He walked in the Nave of the cathedral while the bride heard the mass in the choir.[30] The vain bride pouted, tossed her head, and refused to take Henry as her husband because she loved someone else. Then, Charles IX coolly walked up, placed one hand on her chest and the other on the back of her head and compelled an involuntary nod. The couple was united by the bishop. While she participated in mass, Henry of Navarre, on the arm of Admiral Coligny, was surrounded by musketeers.[31]

On the Isle of Wight, the governor's wife was affected by this marriage because it started bloodshed. A bell at the Hotel de Ville called the citizens to arms, and the battle raged. The fury of despair grew out of the feud between the house of Guise and the Catholics, and the house of Condé and the Huguenots.[32]

Protestants in Paris were against all Catholics--Spanish, French, English. The women and children who found passage on packet boats to Devonshire, loved freedom with a passion, and never forgave the Catholic insults.[33]

On Sunday, 24 August 1572, the feast of St. Bartholomew was celebrated in spite of the prevailing spirit of hatred. Two minutes after midnight an alarm bell sounded from the tower of the Palace of Justice. Men shouting, "Vive Dieu et le roi," forced Admiral Coligny's door at the Louvre and stabbed him. They threw his body out the window.[34]

When bullets and daggers cut down men, women and children of the Protestants, armed troops began to exterminate all enemies of the Church of Rome. However, a number of Huguenot noblemen, lodged on the south side of the Seine

River, and English soldiers Walter Raleigh, Humphrey Gilbert and others hid at the embassy of Sir Francis Walsingham.[35]

On St. Bartholomew's Day the massacre extended to all provinces. Alarms rang from steeple to steeple, city to hamlet, valley to hillside. People defended themselves with their own arms, until most Protestants were killed or jailed. Fugitives from Bretagne, Normandy, and Picardy fled to the English islands of Jersey, Guernsey, the Isle of Wight, and to England or Scotland.[36] Six or seven thousand were slaughtered.

On 10 September 1572, the devastating news of the three-day massacre of Huguenots in Paris circulated in France and England. The beloved leader Admiral Coligny was villainously murdered.[37] Henry of Navarre refused to abjure the Protestant faith and led groups of his friends in hand-to-hand fighting.

The governor's wife on the Isle of Wight continued to play the ongoing, unsavory role as a peacemaker between French and English merchants.[38] In 1573, Sir Edward Horsey, ambassador to the court of France, pled the cause of Rochelle and the French Protestants. There, the peace between the King and the Huguenots was attributed to his understanding, and that of his wife, of the situation.

In May 1573, the governor's wife failed to understand the lax morals of the English circle of her husband's intimate friends, especially Robert Dudley, Earl of Leicester. Dudley's rumored love for the Queen Elizabeth, and his scheme of marrying Her Majesty failed.[39] Currently, at Esher, Governor Horsey's wife was requested to witness a secret marriage at night between Dudley and the widow, Douglas Sheffield. And, in the English court, the governor's wife was involved in the legal dispute involving bribery that had disgusting details. She courageously faced her uncertain legal status--a French wife married to an English member of parliament.[40] In 1580, Edward and the Dutchman, Cornelius Stevenson, from Knox's Church in Geneva, set up works for gunpowder, and the manufacture of saltpeter. The governor's wife turned her eyes the other way,[41]

Upon her visit in Normandy, Mademoiselle learned that Edward also had a wife alive in France, and he kept another island house with the rich widow. This news stopped his marrying the widow. The governor's wife made the difficult

Chapter 6: Mademoiselle Horsey

decision to leave Edward and to return to her beach home in Normandy.[42]

In 1583, his ex-wife returned to the Isle of Wight to read the epitaph over his effigy in armor that was under the marble canopy in Newport Church. She reviewed their strange life together, their years devoted to the Protestant project, and efforts towards the wildlife preservation in the New Forest on the island. She concluded Sir Edward had performed excellent services for Queen Elizabeth.

Although, as substitute governor she had given over seventeen years of good service to the Protestant cause on the Isle of Wight, and squarely faced debates about women's rights, she boarded a nameless ship for Normandy. This little known woman, preferred to remain anonymous in history. The governor's wife took back her maiden form of address, "Mademoiselle", to speak to fleets from Darracott Hall Kent, sailing from the Channel Islands to Montevideo.

Mademoiselle moved back to here original home in Normandy and watched the ships sail for the New World.

Mary Queen of Scots. Unknown artist.
By Courtesy of National Portrait Gallery, London.

Jane Dudley Grey. Unknown artist.
By Courtesy of National Portrait Gallery, London.

Margaret Countess of Cumberland, by Lawrence Hilliard.
By Courtesy of Victoria and Albert Museum, London..

Elizabeth Throckmorton, Lady Raleigh.
By Courtesy of The Colonial Williamsburg Foundation.

Baptism of Virginia Dare.
A Popular History of the United States, John Clark Ridpath.

Chapter 7
MARGARET RUSSELL CLIFFORD, Countess of Cumberland
(1560 - 1616)

Generous contributions from Margaret, Countess of Cumberland, established safe ports for the Royal Navy. Meg was the youngest child of Sir Francis Russell, Earl of Bedford and Lord Lieutenant of Devon and Cornwall, and Margaret St. John, of Bledso. Her grandfather, the second Earl of Bedford, instructed Admiral Winter's fleet to capture the Channel Islands in the name of England. When Meg was born during the turmoil in 1560, her father's ward was young George Clifford, and his godson was fifteen-year-old Francis Drake, of Crowndale.

According to the activities recorded by her daughter, Anne, in the *Diary of Lady Anne Clifford,* Meg exerted a powerful influence for goodness in the Age of Elizabeth I. During the settlements in the New World, she influenced the voyages of Clifford and Drake, and she became a friend of Dr. John Dee. She remade commerce in England, and her generous contributions enabled trade to be carried on in the East Indies. She also participated in state affairs and contributed to the finances of the modern England.

Before Meg's birth in 1560, her father attended Protestant conferences at Cambridge concerning the sacrament, and he witnessed the crowning of Jane Grey. After encouraging the Courtenay uprising in the West, Lord Russell was imprisoned. And when he escaped he fled to Zurich, and he sent money to Protestants in prison. Before Elizabeth I became queen, he kept in close touch with the reforming party that studied geography, arithmetic, and science, and he joined the "secret cabinet" preparations for further reformation of the English Church.[1] His children were encouraged to recognize the benefits of the Protestant religion. Lord Russell became the perfect royal servant to Queen Elizabeth.

The young child, Meg, was included in the Russell caravan of Marian exiles as they rode from Tavistock manor past the tree-lined entrance of Buckland Abbey, in South Devon. They were on route to discuss politics and religion at Powderham Castle, owned by the Lords Courtenay, of the de Rivers family. The coastal road along the Exe River led to Exeter, the capital of Western England, that was recognized as an important center of trade with the Greeks and Phoenicians.[2]

The Charter for the incorporation of the Merchants Adventurers of the City of Exeter, granted by Queen Mary in 1556, was regranted by Queen Elizabeth. The stone tablet in Bartholomew Yard read, "Azure a Castle Or standing on the Waves of the Sea proper, in two ducal Crowns d'Or." The arms of merchant adventurers were on either side of the arms of the city of Exeter, capitol of South Devon.[3]

The greatness of Elizabethan England was due in the past to tithes paid by Exeter members under the magnificent stained glass windows of Exeter Cathedral. Representatives from the boroughs Hayes Barton, Westward Ho, Bideford, Northam, Darracott, and Barnstaple from North Devon joined families from South Devon. And, Bishop of Exeter, Miles Coverdale, completed Tyndall's translation of the Bible.[4]

The Guildhall of Society of Merchants encouraged trading with royalty in France and Spain, and they adopted laws in the Guildhall permitting them to influence communities. In 1560, Exeter city fathers took a great step forward in foreign trade, as they set out to build the expensive canal from Exeter to the sea. With the foundation laid for England's great challenge to Spain for the mastering of the sea, these merchants became acquainted with the coasts of the West Indies Islands and the Spanish Main.[5]

The Russell family had few peers in the provinces, and was among the privileged top stratus of Exeter society who had the opportunity to amass a fortune. They maintained public order, organized defense, and provided for the poor. The Exeter canal enabled them to found new markets.[6] Merchants traded from Exeter and Dartmouth in wool, tin, and fish. The wine vault bordered on the quay, and their woolen goods were sent to France by way of Guernsey, a Channel Island where the merchants had close family ties. Wealth was concentrated in the hands of a few in the top stratus of Exeter society.

The French-English partnership for Bordeaux wines had existed with traders since the marriage in 1152 of Eleanor of Acquitaine with Henry, Duke of Anjou, who became Henry II, King of England in 1154. This Vintners' Company traded to St.John-de-Luz, where the merchants learned from the Basques about the profits of cod and whale in Newfoundland.[7] The Vintners' Company, one of the twelve great Livery Companies, also participated in the election of the Lord Mayors of London, Barnstaple, and other cities.

When Francis Drake returned from Caribbean and the West Indies Islands, he pointed to the location of Drake's Channel on his map. Drake detailed incidents to Meg's family about his search for Spanish prize ships from a mountain top seat on St. Thomas Island. And, he shared his reconnaissance work and the crew's relaxation on Negril Beach, Jamaica. He described the emerald-blue waters surrounding the San Blas Islands, where he climbed a tree on the Isthmus of Panama to view the Pacific Ocean.

When Meg was twelve years old, her parents supported Drake's ships that captured the Spanish town Nombre de Dios, Isthmus of Panama, and crossed the territory to the Pacific Ocean. Samples of his loot of gold and silver mined high in the Andes and transported by mule trains across the Isthmus of Panama, stimulated the sustaining interest of the Earl of Bedford and the Countess for further ventures.

One draft plan sanctioned by Queen Elizabeth granted Drake permission to sail through the Straits of Magellan and around the world to China, establishing forts along the route. Seventeen-year-old Meg and George Clifford invested in the *Golden Hind,* the *Elizabeth,* and three small ships for Drake's 1577 voyage.

These vessels sailed through the Straits of Magellan, across the Pacific and Indian Oceans, to England. For this around-the-world voyage, Drake was knighted by the Queen.[8] And, Meg took a special interest in trade from Sutton Pool to foreign lands.

According to 1577 Plymouth records, "In this yere Francs, Erle of Bedforde, the Countess his wife, the Earl of Cumberland, the L:Norris, the L:Wharton accompanied with divers other gent of good word come twise to this towne, and here received at the townes charge."[9]

Margaret, at seventeen, was given in marriage to George Clifford, Lord Russell's ward from the north who was a buccaneer on a maritime route. Meg's wedding to nineteen-year-old Clifford took place by invitation from Queen Elizabeth in Her court on 24 June 1577.[10] Immediately afterwards, the couple left behind the sophisticated culture of the south. They traveled over tracks and moors to the frozen north where the groom's late father, Henry Clifford, had owned acres of pastures and farmlands, two almshouses, seven churches and chapels. The rough castles Appleby, Brougham, Pendragon, Brough, and Barden also had been his property.[11] The grooms's grandfather, minister Henry Percy, 1st Earl of Northumberland, had been executed in the era of Bloody Mary, because he was the first supporter of Calvinism. According to the *Diary of Lady Anne Clifford*, following the long journey, Meg's caravan reached Cliffords' sturdy, almost inaccessible Norman castle of Skipton, in Craven, in the province of Yorkshire near Scotland. From the tower at Skipton Castle, Meg looked at their water supply running through the conduit court, and wondered how it was possible for the castle to be sturdily built on a rock with a river flowing 200 feet below.[12]

In the patriarchal fashion typical of cool northern hospitality, Lady Anne Dacre received her son's wife under the Clifford coat of arms. This manner of greeting was used in the province, and at Skipton. Uncomfortable in the atmosphere of the north, Meg turned her attention to lace-making and straw-platting. She yearned for the excitement of Plymouth, Dartmouth and Exeter, and for the straightforward answers of the people she loved.[13] Meg settled to live peacefully at this castle in the north.

When Lady Anne Dacre died four years later, twenty-one-year-old Lady Margaret became a suitable, remarkable mistress for the many castles. She fell heir to supervising the legacy of Henry Clifford's fortune and his vast estates. With determination and expertise and her natural wit, she managed tenants and servants.

Chapter 7: Margaret Russell Clifford

Adept in keeping accounts and in business matters, she was frugal. In the diary, it appeared Meg was born to rule over households, including those of her mother-in-law. Meg's charming and affectionate husband lived the life of a country gentlemen. Clifford, known as the third Earl of Cumberland, loved horse racing and gambling. The couple enjoyed each other and were on excellent terms. Meg became pregnant twice within the year, and adored her children. She taught her precocious boys to sit straight, to walk with shoulders back and chin in, and to recite the Protestant catechism for children. Meg's affection for her husband shone in her eyes until tragedies shattered their happiness. Their five-year-old son fell ill with a dreadful fever and, in spite of excellent nursing, died. Within two years their sturdy, eldest son passed away in a farm accident. Meg was stunned beyond belief.

During this stressful time from 1586 onwards, Cumberland's life was "one long record of adventure and absence." According to Meg, the Earl "exchanged country pleasures with new thoughts of greater worlds."[14]

The portrait in the National Portrait Gallery depicts Lady Clifford, Countess of Cumberland, at the age of twenty-five in a gorgeous lace fluted collar, pearls and a tiara. In the stiff clothes, she was dutiful and prim in the presence of elders, and she was dignified and exact in pious observances.[15]

The financiers in 1585 of John Davis included Sir Francis Russell, the Earl of Cumberland and his wife Lady Cumberland. Davis, of Sandbridge, made three voyages to the Artic Seas in search of a northwest passage. An Inuit Indian dressed in fur and carrying snow shoes, a stick, and a bird on his shoulder had returned to England with Davis. And, the Exeter financiers learned about the polar bears, loons, and sea nymphs among the icebergs. The third voyage to explore Northern America for a route to Cathay was sponsored by wealthy Exeter citizens. Off the coast of Labrador, on the last voyaage, he discovered the strait which bears his name. Davis Strait was from one hundred eighty to five hundred miles wide. This Strait had soundings exceeding five thousand feet in the northern and southern portions but not reaching two thousand five hundred feet in the intervening region. A sheet of water separated Greenland on the east from land on the west, and Baffin's Bay connected with the Atlantic. There were two powerful currents, one on the west towards the south and one on the east, towards the north. The northern half of Davis Strait was navigable only in late summer.[16]

Meg's husband became determined to sail around the world. Supported by his wife and the Russell family, the Earl embarked on a cruise to capture Spanish ships. He sailed southwestward beyond the mouth of the river Plate, until his crew balked at risking their lives in the Straights of Magellan. The Earl returned without enough success to repay the cost of the expedition.

In 1588 he commanded the Queen's ship *Elizabeth Bonadventure* against the Spanish Armada, and Her Majesty was pleased with the reports of his gallantry. Then, the next year the Queen's ship and six others equipped at his expense were victorious. This fleet unexpectedly captured the Spanish West Indian fleet. Although the Earl's ships ran short of water, and men were reduced to an allowance of spoonfuls of vinegar a day, and some "drank themselves to death with salt water," the Earl kept his temper. He endured the distress of the seamen, and savored the victory over the Spanish fleet.[17]

When he returned home, the Earl was a changed man, and their marriage was slipping. Meg suffered from his cruel jokes. She realized he possessed a muddle-headed will and a mind full of galleons. He chose to buccaneer on the dangerous, pirate-infested maritime routes by plundering towns and capturing prize ships. In 1589, the Russell family, including Meg's husband, joined Exeter merchants and supported Don Antonio of Portugal.

The Earl was little more than a buccaneer upon the maritime trade routes of France and Spain when their only daughter Anne was born in 1590. At this time, Meg's husband was absent at sea upon one of the many voyages he undertook "for the service of Queen Elizabeth, for the good of England and of his own person." Much in her sea-captains disturbed Elizabeth, and it was not adventure alone that troubled Her Majesty. Naturally, Meg turned into an ever-present mother for her only child, Anne.[18] Meg also invested in the Earl of Cumberland's expedition in 1591. When the Queen's ship *Garland* and seven others sailed to Costa Rico, the Canaries, and coasts of Spain, they captured valuable prizes that were recaptured. At the Azores, the Earl sent a ship to warn Sir Thomas Howard of the powerful

Chapter 7: Margaret Russell Clifford

Spanish Armada ready to attack the English.[19]

In June 1592 Meg and her sisters investing with the Earl, furnished another costly expedition. With other ships, he captured the great carrack *Madre de Dios*. When this claim was legally decided against the Earl, the Queen allotted him a sum of thirty-six thousand pounds. That autumn, the Earl spent the entire time at court attending the Queen. And, Her Majesty applauded when he received the degree of Master of Arts at Oxford, and when he was made a Knight of the Garter. Neither Meg nor her sisters received their share of the loot of this venture.

Meg suffered a severe shock when the Earl appeared in the tilt yard as the Knight of Pendragon dressed in golden armor. His visor was lowered, and lance was in hand, as were "plumes and pendants all as white as snow." He wore a pointed diamond ring, and the queen's glove imbedded with diamonds in his hat.[20] Since the exchanging of gloves signified a marriage agreement, according to well-known English mores, Meg felt there was no need for the Earl to pursue such a life.

His wife received a sympathetic letter from Her Majesty commending the Earl of Cumberland's spirit of dangerous adventure. Meg recognized the great wickedness on earth, and prayed hours on her knees for her husband to find grace in the eyes of the Lord for his long record of absence from home. The Earl roamed the seas summer and winter in the service of Queen Elizabeth for the "good of England and of his own person." Meg hoped he would return to her, and she studied the tone of the Queen's letter, as well as Her Majesty's temper and appearance. The pale face, miserable health and fiery blood indicated courage was dear to her Majesty. Meg concluded The Queen favored the Earl with more than tolerance and secret delight, and the Earl stood in high favor with the Queen. The true fact surfaced--the loot of the Spanish seas flattered the Queen.[21]

Meg, known as Lady Cumberland, inherited the chore of keeping records of the great Clifford fortune. She contributed from her personal wealth to furnishing carracks and galleons for eleven voyages, including the one involving Don Antonio of Portugal. While her husband squandered money on wild living, Meg was frugal with small expenditures.[22]

She had comprehensive knowledge about the ships she sponsored at sea.

When this squadron fought and burned the great carrack *Ciuco Llagas* worth 2,000 pounds, the Earl became ill. Meg consulted the details of the lengthy list of catalogues of treasure unloaded on the quay at Plymouth and Dartmouth. This included "mother-of pearl, porcelain dishes, raw silk, spices, elephants' tusks, turkey carpets, quilts, jewels. . . small diamonds, rubies, great diamonds, orient pearls, pieces of gold, gold rings."[23] Thieves pilfered unattended spoil and made off with booty into the great western moors. Afterwards, the Earl was appointed Lord Lieutenant of Cumberland, territory located in the far north bordering Scotland, and he became a member of the Queen's privy council.[24]

Meg, Countess of Cumberland, studied the properties of plants and flowers, distilled herbs for medicinal purposes, and she dabbled in alchemy. She visited the alchemist Dr. John Dee, to learn about the geography and the dangers her husband was subjected to at sea. The distinguished professor so approved of Meg and her high standards that she was invited to serve as godmother for Dee's young daughter, Margaret. The countess was courteous to all sorts of people.[25]

For solace, Anne's mother carried her prayer book to the rose garden and read aloud to her daughter from the *Book of Job* about the sad plight of people in Job's day. Stern principles of religion were implanted in the child.[26] These included Calvin's comments on St. Paul's advice, "Meditate carefully on the truth. . .it is as a precious metal that must be proved in the fire. . . for if you feel weaker than you ought to be as the tree planted by the waterside which with its living roots, shall never perish between the storms that are upon it. Harden yourself, dear lady, against the frown of the world. If you do good, this is the reward promised us from above."[27]

Because the countess was excluded from her husband's life, their daughter Anne was strictly raised and severely restrained by her mother. For the child's party, Meg had bought feathers for hair, green stockings, and a mask. However, while hired musicians played, Anne overate on fruit until she fell ill. Meg insisted Anne keep in a notebook meticulous accounts including the precise names of servants and messengers and their little rewarding presents. Consequently, the governess, and the tutor, and the poet remained respectful. Anne chose good books,

Chapter 7: Margaret Russell Clifford

virtuous companions, good thoughts. Her activity time was budgeted by the hourglass. Together, mother and daughter visited the feudal castles on northern estates, and made southern visits among cousins whose opinions of stately aunts and about the endeavors of the crown colored the conversations.[28]

In January 1598, the Earl of Cumberland undertook the most considerable of all his expeditions. During his proposal to establish an English settlement where Drake had failed, he fitted out some twenty ships at his own cost, and sailed from Plymouth. His crews plundered ships near the Canaries and rested at Dominica. On 6 June 1598, these ships fell in full force on Puerto Rico and made themselves masters of San Juan. The Earl proposed to clear this island of Spaniards and establish it as an English settlement. However, when violent sickness broke out among the troops, he abandoned the project.[29]

The earl encountered every kind of danger from sickness, battles, thirst, and weather. The diary read, "avoiding no part of distress that others, even the meanest endured, his spirit remained...higher than the winds."[30] He was rarely sick, though his deceitful letters to Meg were interlaced with description of sickness, thirst and weather. He established the important base at Puerto Rico that made it safe for Royal Navy ships to dock in the New World.

In 1601, when she subscribed to the East Indian Company, the earl called Meg, "Protestant Countess of the Royal Navy." This title she abhorred. Within two decades, more than sixty-seven West Indies Company ships rounded the coast of Africa to China. Commodities from eighty-seven ports were brought to Lisbon. The East Indian Company was successful.[31]

In the spring of 1603, Meg attended the body of Queen Elizabeth, as it was carried from Whitehall Palace with great solemnity to Westminster. After the Queen's funeral on Thursday, 8 April 1603, Anne wrote, "The lords and ladies going on foot to attend it, my Mother and my Aunt of Warwick being mourners, but I was not allowed to be one, because I was not high enough, which did much trouble me then, but I stood in the church at Westminster to see the solemnities performed." Standing quite close with Anne during the funeral service, the Countess shared her mixed emotions concerning her husband and the Queen.[32]

According to the Diary, "A little after this my Lady and a great deal of other company... went down with my Aunt Warwick to North Hall and from thence we all went to Tibbals to see the King (James) who used my Mother and aunt very graciously, but we all saw a great change in the fashion of the Court as it is now and of that in the Queen's time, for we were all (infested with lice) by sitting in the chamber of Sir Thomas Erskine. As the King came out of Scotland, when he lay at York, there was a strife between my Father and Lord Burleigh (who was the President), who should carry the sword, but it was adjudged on my Father's side because it was an office by inheritance and so it lineally descended to me."[33]

About attempting to overtake Aunt Warwick, Anne's Diary stated, "My Mother and I...killed three horses that day with extremity of heat." Later, "The first time I ever saw the Queen (Anne of Denmark) and Prince Henry... she kissed us all and used us kindly." At Althrop, the Queen favored Lady Hatton and Lady Cecil, and showed no favor to the elderly ladies, but to Lady Rich and such like company.[34]

From there, the Court removed to Grafton and banqueted with great royalty. The King and Queen were entertained with speeches and delicate presents. "At this time my Mother was there, but not held as mistress of the house, by reason of the difference between my Lord and her, which was grown to a great height."[35]

Meg used many coaches to follow the Queen's train. She even rode horseback to see the daughter of King James and Queen Anne. At Windsor, Anne stood next to Elizabeth's Grace in the shrine of the great hall while the King and all the knights sat at dinner with favorite lords and younger ladies. Here Meg looked like a ghost that wanted the soul of comfort.[36]

When the group moved to Hampton Court, Anne and her Mother "lay in one of the round towers, round about which were tents where they died two or three a day of the plague. There I fell extremely sick of a fever." Meg attended King James about the business of Anne's father and her. And, the Earl followed his suit about the Border lands to the King. Anne went often to the Queen and Lady Arbella Stuart.[37]

Eleven-year-old Anne colored her hair daily. She wrote, "Sometimes my

Chapter 7: Margaret Russell Clifford

mother and he did meet, when their countenance did show the dislike they had one of the other, yet he would speak to me in a slight fashion and give me his blessing."[38] Meg's child was full of sadness.

The King and Queen were crowned at Westminster on 15 July 1603. Meg and the Earl attended in their robes, and their countenances plainly showed dislike for each other.[39]

The Earl suffered remorse and depression when he contracted a fatal illness, and wrote on his death bed to "sweet and dear Meg", begging forgiveness for the wrongs he had done her.[40] When he died on 30 October 1605, he was 1,000 pounds in debt, and there were problems at Westmoreland. His northern estates were bequeathed to his brother, Sir Francis Clifford, with possible reversion to Anne, the natural inheritor.[41] And, this triggered trouble for Meg.

In 1605, Anne wrote to Meg about the distressing facts concerning her own forthcoming marriage: "I have had a great deal of talk with My Lord (presumably her father) about that matter you know of, for that match, and My Lord hath promised me that there shall nothing pass for any match whatsoever, but that your consent should be asked as a chief matter. I beseech your Ladyship to pardon my boldness in writing to you thus rudely, and to let nobody know of these matters, though they may be but trifling.

"I rest, as I am bound by nature, love and duty,

Your ladyship's most obedient and dutiful daughter,

Anne Clifford"[42]

Several years later, Meg witnessed the sad event of Anne's marriage. At nineteen Anne was married 25 February 1609 in Meg's chambers in Augustine Fryers, London, to twenty-year-old Richard Sackville, Earl of Dorset, a companion of Prince Henry's. The temperament of Anne's husband, gaming and squandering his money, was similar to her father's.[43] Meg planned to visit them.

When Meg drove through the marble pillars of Knole and Wilton, in Wiltshire, to visit her daughter, she encountered the falconer, footmen, bird watchers, and many servants. She called the places "gay arbors of anguish."[44] She longed for the good people of the West Country and the mecca of business at

Plymouth, and she dreamed of Westmoreland. Meg counted her grandchildren. Among Anne's five children was Lady Margaret, named for Meg, but called "The Child," because of the strife between Anne and her husband. Too weak to enter additional disputes, Meg departed for Westmoreland in the North, where a cold chillness turned to heat and pain in her side. In January 1616, after Anne consoled Lady Raleigh in the Tower, she departed to visit Meg at Westmoreland. Anne traveled with twenty-six horsemen and four coaches northward over the Clifford lands she was destined to inherit. With her ladies-in-waiting and her servants, Meg's daughter rode in a great coach in the middle of a long procession, carrying bedding, chairs, carpets and fresh curtains. Lurching and lumbering up and down hills, she journeyed to churches, chapels, almshouses and decaying castles, and directed horsemen over lonely roads between moors and fields, over bridges, into rough, wild country, dim with dust and full of boulders. Anne scrutinized the countryside through the window, while women opposite her clutched sliding bags and baskets. They careened over roads no coach had been known to pass.

Anne wrote, if she must die, "it was the same thing to die in the way as in her house, in her litter as in her bed."[45]

When she arrived at Westmoreland, Anne and Meg lay together talking of trends and laws of her Mother's times. Obviously, the land settlements involved in the inheritance of the vast estates would eventually be taken to King James for settlement. Meg mellowed, and blamed her money for the Earl's unfaithfulness. When Meg's side opened, there was a hideous, incurable abscess.

On her desk at Brougham, Westmoreland, in the same chamber where the Earl was born,[46] lay an almost tragic account of Meg's life divided into sevenths, each seventh more disastrous than the one preceding it. She admitted a brief oasis of happiness during her teens, but quickly turned to a note of sorrow. After she died 24 May 1616, her body, sent in her own coach, was accompanied by about forty men and women on horseback to Appleby, and put in the ground.[47]

Meg's contributions had enormously helped trade and Protestant settlements in foreign lands. She was responsible for remaking commerce in England. The generosity of Meg to the East Indies Company enabled trade to be carried on around the world. All her life, Meg had a "powerful influence for goodness over her posterity."[48]

Chapter 8
MARY ST. LEGER GRENVILLE
(c1542 - 1623)

Mary St. Leger, wife of Richard Grenville, and eldest daughter and heiress of John St. Leger and Catherine Neville, was born at "Annery," Bideford, Devon. Her bravery and courage, mentioned in the annals of Ireland, helped her survive personal hardship, tragedy and war. Mary dealt successfully with Irish soldiers, Spanish prisoners, and French refugees. She contributed to the Great Plan to Conquer the World, and assisted in voyages to Labrador, Newfoundland, and Roanoke Island on the American coast.[1]

St. Mary's Church, Bideford, a Saxon church, was the legal benefice of an advowson bestowed on Richard de Greville in 1083. And, the Maltese Cross with Virgin and Child chiseled in the stonework of Bideford Bridge was donated by a Grenville in memory of the Knights of the Order of St. John. Sir Richard Grenville, son of a Cornish soldier who drowned 8 March 1545 in the sinking of the *Mary Rose*, performed notable service for England. Kin to royalty, to Sir Walter Raleigh, and West Country gentlemen, the Grenville name was spelled in various ways such as Greenfield, Granville, and Grinville.[2]

These families pledged episcopal indulgences to upkeep the wondrous bridge over the Torridge River where people drowned in wild water. Bridge benefactors at the church dinners were tithers, and potters fashioned vases and dishes as contributions. From the rope walk on the quay, members watched a seventy-foot barque pass under the center opening of the twenty-four dissimilar arches of the long, narrow edifice. The bridge shook at the slightest step of a horse in the sheet of shifting sand, and slid downstream each night until an angel pointed to a preacher a sure foundation. This is why church members considered Bideford Bridge "an inspired bridge, a soul-saving bridge, an alms-giving bridge, and an educational bridge."[3]

During the turbulent times of the Reformation, although qualified by blood to join noblewomen at court functions, Mary remained in seclusion. She learned the rudiments of sailing a square-masted barque in rough seas off Devonshire coast. The lessons included the necessity to wait for St. Margaret's Church bells to ring the exact time to sail off a wave over Barnstaple Bar. On the main loop of the moorland coastal road Mary limited her travel past Northam Church and dangerous limestone caves along the steep banks. She observed larkspur, vegetable and herb gardens near Kilkhampton, Stowe, Darracott, Clovelly and Hartland Point. Fennel flowers were brewed for sore eyes, and goat's rue in ale was a safeguard against the plague, and chamomile was used for headaches. Workers twisted hemp while smiths pursued ship crafts, and the cordwainer at Appledore fashioned soldier's boots.[4]

Despite thick autumn fogs and gale force winds from the Atlantic, fishing fleets from France, Spain, and Portugal gathered in coves where underwater rocks claimed many lives. Each summer Bideford seamen, with the aid of John Cabot's 1497 map, sailed through tempestuous seas for Newfoundland. Few ships reached these banks in fifty-three degree north latitude.[5]

The marriage of Mary St. Leger to Sir Richard Grenville, arranged by her parents, took place before 1565, near the Maltese Cross in St. Mary's Church.[6] The bride exercised her options and rights according to the law, "If, after the bargain (of marriage), he takes up a new trick of circumnavigation, (a wife) may let him go where he lift, and (she may) tarry at home when she will."[7]

The groom, a man of the sword, used a charming manner when he kissed his wife and caressed her hair with strong, vigorous hands. His mouth, usually as firm as granite, took on a quality of sweetness, and his silky beard tickled her chin. The couple had three known sons--Bernard, John, and Roger--and five daughters--Mary, Catherine, Ursula, Bridget, and Rebecca.[8]

Chapter 8: Mary St. Leger Grenville

The groom fostered education at Burrough with "his cup of malmasey before him and the lute to which he had been singing laid across his knees while the western sun streamed in upon his high blond forehead and soft, curling locks." Sacrificing some rights while riding the moorland road to Stowe, he developed a thriving existence by infusing new life into the countryside. Every woman ran to her door to look at this typical West Country squire until he became the pride of North Devonshire.[9] Occasionally stern and harsh, this hot-blooded man of the world loved the associations of war and had fearful fits of rage when he saw cowardice or falsehood in sailors. More a soldier than a seaman, Grenville supplied Admiral Coligny with recognizance to several forts in the West Indies.[10]

Mary was aware of the scorched earth policy in Munster, Ireland, where she visited cousin Warham St. Leger in Castle St. Leger. For their children, the Grenvilles acquired Kerrycurrihy estate near Cork. Here, death was expected among rich and poor, and Irish tenants hated the French name St. Leger. They jeered and laughed at the ladies who were unable to cope with the Irish way of life. French Protestant problems were caused by animosity of Catholics whose churches were more popular than the Presbyterian one. They detested Grenville's cruel decisions and this colonization project on their land. Life was cheap and violent.[11] Grenville recommended soldiers should poison women who were sworn enemies of Queen Elizabeth. Persons with leprosy and enemies of the peace wailed and raged, and considered the English soldiers unchristianlike. Shepherds in the meadow dreaded danger from men and wolves. Underfed cattle grazed where wheat, barley, and oats were planted. The odor of bundles of dried sea kelp decaying in puddles, wafted across slimy water. The naked harvesters swinging scythes, knives and hoes, worked near children digging for clams. In the wood carnage in forts of shaking bog, the women warming themselves crept on all fours, awaited a soldier and cupid. If an honest man fell prey to their enticing, they loosened the reins of his horse. If a soldier fell asleep, he was awakened with a poisoned toad or crocodile in his bed. If he wandered into the snare of wild nymphs, death was fast.[12]

On Ireland's southern shore Grenville, Sheriff of Cork, had incorporated the fishing grounds, Baltimore, into a fishing town. After seizing a number of farms in this neighborhood, Sir Warham St. Leger, Sir Humphrey Gilbert, and the sheriff sailed to London to ensure the Queen's approval of this project.[13]

During the owners' absence, when war fever escalated, rebels swore never to depart from Cork unless the mayor delivered up Mrs. Grenville and Lady Ursula St. Leger. The brazen rebel James Fitzmaurice, hunting young women, led four thousand rioting soldiers of fortune to this estate. Men at this castle were beheaded. Tenants in tiny houses, servants, and farm laborers had throats cut, and ten thousand cattle were driven off into hills. The ladies Mary and Ursula wrote an urgent letter requesting help from Lord Deputy Sir Henry Sidney during the crisis. The St. Leger farm was spoiled, and occupants who kept fires burning in the manor endured the cruelties and theft from neighboring castles.[14]

Fearing abduction when rebels attacked her home, Mary performed sailor's duties aboard the schooner *St. Leger* on 14 June 1569. Her children heaved anchor and hastily loosened the sails for their mother to sail the schooner across the rough Irish sea to Bideford. Then the English squires returned with the sheriff, pursued the rebels, and put down rebellions in Munster. The safety of Cork was secured before the family schooner sailed. Sir Warham St. Leger and Grenville financed and established Ulster settlements with colonists from Devon and Cornwall.[15]

The Mayor of Cork, an Irish chieftain, commended Mary for bravery and uncommon courage in his letter of apology. This explicitly stated, "The traitors are not contented to spoil the kine (cows) and horses. . .The men come naked to this city and capture honest housewives of the country, torment them with cruel pains, and execute them."[16]

In April 1570, Mary suspected her husband had Catholic tendencies, and she helped him change his thinking to conform with that of Protestants. As a result, Grenville declared before justices of Cornwall that he was a Protestant. And, he submitted to the Act of Uniformity of Common Prayer and Service in the Church, and offered his services to the Christian cause.

Grenville commanded the the oared galley, *Castle of Comfort* that joined raging battles between Christians and heathens in the Mediterranean near the Island of Malta. This 240-ton privately financed warship, equipped with powerful armament and victualed by Mary and other ladies, fought at Lepanto. When Christians won the victory over the heathen Turks, Queen Elizabeth wrote to the Bishop of London to officially ordain 8 November 1571 as a day of solemn Thanksgiving. When Grenville returned he was knighted for bravery in last battle of the crusades.[17]

When Mary boarded the *Castle of Comfort,* two-hundred-fifty black and white oarsmen, five to a bench with possessions beneath, stood. Discomfort was obvious. When they leaned forward, and sat in unison, faces reflected a hell where rest was unknown. Speaking in Spanish, Mary generated feelings of security and relief from war among these prisoners, and they willingly adventured to foreign shores.

When serving as justice of the peace and representative of Cornwall in Parliament, Grenville and Mary financed the joint stock Cathay Company composed of gentlemen, knights, aldermen, and nobles. They proposed to sail via the North-West Passage to trade with China and the western coast of America. Each stockholder owned a partial share of six thousand pounds, divided into two hundred forty shares to furnish and to send ships to Cathay. Husbands and wives with letters patent promised L5,000, viz. L2,000 in shipping and furniture, L2,000 in victuals and necessaries, and L1,000 in cloth and merchandise for trading purposes.

By 2 March 1574 when Huguenot exiles were settling in Devonshire, Grenville made the first practical suggestion for the English Colonial Empire. With Sir Humphrey Gilbert, Sir George Peckham and Christopher Carleill he sought the Queen's permission to embark on an enterprise for discovery. Accompanied by John Martin, Francis Knollys, Sir Walter Raleigh, and Sir Philip Sidney, they petitioned the Queen to colonize rich and unknown lands "reserved for England and for the honor of (Her) Majesty." Then the *Castle of Comfort* sailed from Bideford for unknown lands in the Northwest Passage. William Salterne, inheritor of his grandparents' barques, shared the route fishing boats used to Belle Isle at the mouth of the St. Lawrence River, and north to Red Bank, Labrador. Here, where night was equal to day, and lines and tackling were freezing, mariners found it difficult to handle the sails. With the use of John Cabot's map, and facts about forts, shelters, and whale fishing, stockholders aboard sought a possible site for a colony.[18]

Upon their return, Mary became the first alderman to address an interested audience. For listeners speaking French, she translated the varied spelling on an English document concerning the incorporation of the "Company of Kathai." Her words sounded similar to those in the charter of Grenville's great uncle, Admiral Dudley. Cathay Company members knew the South seas were already explored as far as the La Plata River, mountains near Montevideo, and Magellan's Strait. This plan emphasized that all male children and heirs of patentees were to be admitted gratis. Childless members were empowered to assign shares, and it was lawful to plant settlements in places the Spaniards claimed as their possession. Advantages included enlarging the Christian faith, increasing English navigation and treasure, and setting idle, needy people to work. Prices of spices and goods obtained from the Portuguese and Spaniards would be voided. This endeavor was to conduct gainful commerce with Spanish ports by intimidation, to capture Spanish vessels, and to establish a mainland English settlement that was against the Spanish treasure fleet.[19]

This lady alderman spoke French to carefully interpret the English document to listeners, "There lies the South Sea. You enter it by the Strait of Magellan or by the Portuguese route around the cape. Once there, you have the Mollucas and China on the Western fringe, the beautiful temperate Australia full of gold on the Southern edge, and the Straits of Anian, (if you can find them) to leave it by the north."[20]

Grenville planned a summer departure to reach Magellan's Strait before 21 September 1574. After exploring the islands and fortifications, he expected to arrive at the Straits of Anian (Bering Strait), and to plat every bay, road, port, channel and perilous places. Forts in permanent cities with would cope with the Spanish. Men would discover new trades. They could market Devon cloth, intercept Spanish treasure, and locate gold mines. Precious merchandise including gold, silver, pearls, and rich grain would belong to colonists. Upon his return from the northern seas in summer, men would be employed to traffic with Cathay. Loud

Chapter 8: Mary St. Leger Grenville 103

applause followed the feminine interpretation of the Plan to Conquer the World.[21]

Queen Elizabeth granted this license for the Company of Kathai. Richard Grenville, Piers Edgecombe, Arthur Bassett, John Fitz, Edmund Tremayne, William Hawkins, Alexander Arundell, Thomas Digges, Martin Dare, Dominick Chester, and "divers others" were empowered to fit out ships for exploring in the dominions of the great Cam of Cathaie.[22]

After Grenville rendered service to Queen Elizabeth for transporting 2,000 soldiers to Ireland, he received the queen's letter of thanks for good conformity. Seven ships, plus the *Castle of Comfort*, were already armed with the avowed intention of a voyage of discovery to Labrador. Since it was too late in the season to start a South Seas voyage, that fleet carried many soldiers and sailors, 500 of them gentlemen, to help Montgomery in Normandy.[23]

On 10 December 1574, Mary, an alderman, translated "The Charter of Incorporation for Bideford" to French carpenters, blacksmiths, and cordwainers from Huguenot ports. Weavers sipping wine gathered on the hill to hear every word. Phrase for phrase in French was followed by silent approval of facts. The free town, Bideford, was to be governed by a mayor elected yearly, five aldermen, and seven capital burgesses. The town was a body politic and one community in deed, fact, and name, forever. "A parishioner may pay any legacy to the pastor by free will to gratify him. . .not obligatory. Every person who comes to be married shall be . . .at liberty to give what he pleases. . ." According to custom, a parishioner never tithed hay. Tithes of apples, pears, beans and peas went through Bideford church to the preacher and to the lord of the manor, Grenville, who owned the advowson.

A weekly market and fairs were in February, July and November. In the Guild Hall a court of records, held every three weeks, studied civil pleas. Some people profited from stolen goods and from the taxes of bread, wine and ale. Polite applause followed the speech.

The civid life of Bideford began after aldermen and burgesses consented to grammar schools near the bake house. Benefactors donated "Grenville House" and "Darracott House." These grammar school buildings for the French Huguenots were constructed on bridge lands. Ten poor children from the workhouse and town were chosen to attend. Children of Protestant refugees were taught reading, writing, English and French, as well as the arts. Annual sports events included races in running and jumping. The listeners hoped to have a mathematical school to educate poor boys of the parish in navigation and qualify them for sea service. William Darracott became customs collector for tolls on the bridge.[24]

The announcement that a portion of the town's revenues was assured brought a resounding approval.

In 1576, the old and new enterprise were interpreted to Westcountrymen. Mr. Grenfield's discourse concerned a Streight in the Northwest Passage to Cathay and the East Indies. This asserted "there is a strait to be entered between Baccalaos and Greenland." This shorter route under the congealed Artic circle had extreme cold, a short open season, and a longer but easier and more certain route than by the Strait of Magellan. Grenville's observation was ". . .after the strait is perfectly discovered it may be safely used. ."[25]

In spite of the fact that the Cathay Company voyage had the Queen's blessing, the license was canceled because the Spanish ambassador doubted Grenville's intentions.

In a letter addressed to "Mr. Grenville" Her Majesty stated she feared Sir Richard's reputation as a "great pirate" would affect Prince Philip of Spain. When the license for the Cathay Company voyage was revoked, it was useless and dangerous for Grenville to argue with the Queen about the difference between piracy and privateering. He regarded the Spaniards as enemies of God and man, and under a commission of the queen, booty taken from them was a lawful prize.

Mary renovated Buckland Abbey, home of former Cistercian monks, which was acquired from the crown by grandfather Grenville. The square tower between the soaring walls of the church was retained, and three floors were built through the length of the old monastery. The nave, the crossing, and the chapel of massive abbey were preserved, and the kitchen was remodeled. The wall of the north transept was removed to give light to the main rooms, and the staircase next to the side walls was supported with beams.

Chapter 8: Mary St. Leger Grenville

The date 1576 was carved over the fireplace mantle in the great hall. And, figures representing justice, temperance, fortitude, and learning, represented cardinal virtues of the Knights of St. John. A contemporary knight rested a horse under a vine as if the world was his field to be ploughed. According to an observer, "The knight has turned his war-horse loose, hung up the shield upon the tree of Life, and, with a skull and a hour-glass beside him, sits quietly meditating upon death and eternity."[26]

Grenville sold Buckland Abbey in January 1580, after he transformed Cornwall into an army camp to defend England. He risked his life to survey the rocky ruins of Tintagel Castle, reputedly the home of King Arthur of the Round Table. Mary heard Grenville's opinion, "The island was a dangerous receptacle for an evil affected person."

Mary and Sir Richard were involved in John Oxenham's voyage to the world's treasure house that proved unequal in maritime daring. On Bideford quay John wore gold chains, earrings, and a red rose in his curls. He knew the route to Nombre de Dios, and across Panama, and was privy to Grenville's plan of 1574 that included a settlement near Montevideo. In a Spanish hat with a Quetzal bird, Oxenham had shouted, "Come along! . . . Who'll make his fortune?

    Oh, who will join, jolly mariners all?
        And who will join, says he, O!
    To fill his pockets with the good red goold,
        By sailing on the sea, O!"

Several Bideford boys sailed with Oxenham via the route to Nombre de Dios, and across Panama. This feat led to the world's treasure house and to planned forts around the world. Jailed in Peru and needing help, Oxenham testified that Grenville had a part in this voyage of discovery.[27]

Francis Drake's voyage to Cathay had taken place! Mary's townhouse was like a tavern on a November morning in 1582 when Drake's ships draped in colorful flags anchored in front. Grooms and serving men ran to and fro to gentlemen, sailors, and the Countess of Bath. Eating and drinking, celebrators gave thanks for the famous seaman's circumnavigation of the globe. Although he was not a participant, Grenville's Great Plan was successful![28]

From January through March 1585, Mary's townhouse in Bideford was headquarters for preparations for Grenville's voyages to areas claimed by King Philip of Spain. Queen Elizabeth approved the establishment of a colony on the Outer Banks of America, between Florida and the North Pole. Nearly a dozen Jesuit missions, or forts, existed along the Florida Coast and up the Eastern seaboard. Also, among the ships' financiers were John Arundell, John Stukeley, a Kendall, a Prideaux, a Courtenay, Anthony Rowse, and a Darracott.[29]

Mary supervised friends and children loading victuals from Bideford and Barnstaple on ships destined for Roanoke Island, Virginia, named for the virgin queen. The plan was for 600 men and 100 colonists to sail under Grenville's command. Hunters contributed cooked goose, pheasant, and venison. Fishermen brought salted fish, and farmers supplied smoked hams. Older children lugged condensed milk, apples, and pears, and tots carried aboard tea, corn, sugar, rice, beans and coffee. Supplies for the colony included salt, juniper, and pine tar. Soldiers armed with bows, axes, and spades boarded the *Roebuck*, the Queen's *Tiger*, Raleigh's *Dorothy*, Winter's *Elizabeth*, a herring boat turned into a shipping bark, and three ships on the Torridge. According to the chart, these ships stopped at Plymouth and departed on 15 April 1585 for the islands in the Canaries.[30]

The news was that Grenville planted a base within striking distance of the plate route. Grenville returned to Plymouth on a Spanish ship during the night. Wines, sugar, and large treasures in gold, pearls, cochineal, and ivory were unloaded on the dock. The prisoners aboard, carrying stones and materials for a building, were chained at dusk. A letter from the mercantile house of Fugger dated 5 August 1585 arrived in England via a captured French prize ship containing loot to be divided among shareholders.[31]

By early August, the first colonists under Ralph Lane returned to England with Drake, leaving a well-supplied party of fifteen or eighteen men in the Roanoke Island fort. On 8 May 1587, a second contingent of 115 settlers in seven or eight ships sailed with additional supplies gathered by Mary, her family, and friends. On this Grenville voyage to Roanoke fort, Governor John White commanded the flagship that bore his daughter Eleanor Dare and her husband Ananias.[32]

Chapter 8: Mary St. Leger Grenville

After shaking hands with mayor John Salterne, accountant-geographer Thomas Hariot, and Governor John White and his family, Mary with Rebecca turned away from Bideford quay. The mother was wearing a black robe and hood trimmed in white fur resembling ermine, and her daughter wore a matching outfit, according to artist Turner.[33]

Thomas Hariot's letter entitled *Brief and True Report of new Found land of Virginia*, was interpreted to listeners by Mary. "There no longer remains any reason for disliking the Virginia project. The air is temperate and wholesome there, the soil is fertile and yields the commodities I have listed, and the voyage over the ocean has been so many times performed that we now know it can be done three times a year in any season. However, Sir Walter Raleigh has been liberal in granting large tracts of land there. The last he has given to any man has been five hundred acres, besides many other aids." The writer recommended taking more English cattle, varieties of fruits, roots, and herbs to the Virginia settlement.[34]

In the fall of 1587, Mary met the first Indian from Virginia who landed on Bideford quay. In this relief ship Governor John White had promised his daughter, Eleanor, to rush food and clothing to the Roanoke colonists. The Red Indian, named Raleigh (or "Rawly") after cousin Sir Walter Raleigh, learned to respond to Mary as she translated English words by signs. Later, he answered her English questions about becoming a Christian. In March 1588, in St. Mary's Church, "Rawly" was baptized in the massive font with a Maltese cross.[35]

Food and clothing necessities for the Roanoke colonists were gathered by church people in two poor ships, the *Brave* and the *Roe* by 28 April 1588, and John White set out for Virginia. When these vessels were attacked by the Spanish, neither of his ships performed the intended voyage to the Virginia settlement.[36]

When an alarming report reached England that the Spanish were coming, Grenville, Commander-in-Chief of Western Defenses, called together a council of war in Parliament to guard the coast. These West Country supporters Thomas Cavendish, Sir Walter Raleigh, Anthony Rowse, and John Darracott, Jr. confirmed the objectives for an open war against Philip of Spain.[37]

Grenville helped secure landing places on the Devonshire coast. Nearby roads in Cornwall were readied for the Queen's troops with war supplies to be transported to ravaged Waterford, Ireland. By March 1588, Mary and her ladies supplied the *Tiger, Galleon Dudley, Virgin God Save Her, John of Barnstaple, Prudence of Barnstaple and* the bark *St. Leger*. Unfortunately, the Grenville ship struck Barnstaple bar.[38] When these supply ships joined Her Majesty's navy, restitution for victuals and supplies was made in the name of the Queen. 700 men in eight of the best equipped ships were sent to Drake by 9 April 1588.[39]

Queen Elizabeth gave the order to stay all the ships in the port towns of the realm. Her Majesty commanded Grenville to forbear to defend England against the Spanish Armada. He was ordered to stay all shipping off the north coast of Devon and Cornwall to convey soldiers to Waterford or Cork. Fireboats were prepared for service in the anticipated war.[40]

In Mary's quarantined household, daughter Rebecca and servant Lawrence developed the plague. The other servants left and wandered about. Hot plasters of myrrh, saffron, and rare spices were applied to sick bodies, and a witches' brew was concocted for bleeding and lancing the buboes. Burned aromatic substances purified the air, and open windows and doors let in sea breezes. On the coastal road, privies were built over the unsanitary river. Wheat was uncut, and oxen and sheep died in hedge rows and in uncultivated fields, and there was invading saltwater. Children kept animals clean, and ate bland meals. To stimulate mental health, mild exercises were taken in open air away from the limestone caves. Floors, boards, mouths and nostrils were sprinkled with vinegar. Nevertheless, Mary's daughter Rebecca and servant Lawrence died of infectious diseases. Few lecturers dared come to Bideford, and a great ignorance seized the town.[41]

On 29 March, 1589, "Rawly, a man of Wyganditoia," was buried in the Grenville aisle of St. Mary's Church.[42]

Grenville arrived home in red stockings and steele-plated armor, with a drawn sword to ward off the pests. To these terrible calamities he reacted dangerously, recklessly, and callously. Spanish prisoners claimed the plague was a divine punishment caused by his greed, blasphemy, luxury, and that he committed the sins of gambling, cursing, and drinking. Squatters took over empty property,

Chapter 8: Mary St. Leger Grenville

and orphans roamed the country side, pillaging, using a pitching fork for arms. Education suffered. People unwilling to allow their children to attend the grammar school attempted to teach them at home. The Grenville manor house and town house deteriorated, and land was retaken by wilderness. Hill farms were turned to pasture for sheep. Property boundaries vanished, and stocks were set up to punish offenders.[43]

Mary was in a state of shock when Grenville hurriedly kissed her, and stepped aboard the *Revenge* in need of victuals, and destined for some fatal blow. He intended Bideford men to be first in the merchant ships in the raging battle with the Spanish Armada. On 17 August 1591, the *Susan* (350) tons, Centurion (300 tons), *Mayflower* (300 tons), *Cherubin* (300 tons), *Margaret and John*, (200 tons) and *Corselet* (200 tons) left Plymouth to assist Lord Thomas Howard. In the Azores, refusing to obey orders to flee with other English ships, Grenville waited for 100 sick Bideford men to come aboard the little ship that had a history of mishaps.[44]

Then the *Revenge* ran between fifty-three mountain-like Spanish ships into the heart of the foe. Men with pikes and muskets from the *San Philip* boarded this little ship all night long. Sir Richard, wounded in the head, and ready to die, called, "Fight on! Fight on!" Forty men were slain on the *Revenge*. Half the rest were maimed for life, and the mast and rigging were lying over the side of the ship.[45]

When Grenville gave orders for the ship to be sunk, Bideford seamen replied, "We have children and wives and we will make the Spanish promise to let us go if we yield."

Spaniards bore Richard to their ship, laid him by the mast, and praised him to his face. He arose to say, "Here die I Richard Grenville, with a joyful and quiet mind, for that I have ended my life as a true soldier ought to do, that hath fought for his country, his queen, his religion, and honor; my soul willingly departing out of this body, leaving behind the everlasting fame of a valiant soldier, having behaved as any is duty bound to do."[46]

Their son testified until his voice broke, about how his father died of wounds and about the sinking of the *Revenge*.[47] The Spanish Armada was defeated in the precipitous rocky gorges in the Irish sea.

In St. Mary's church, Mary Grenville's penetrating eyes searched those of Bideford for forgiveness. Parishioners remembered her religious zeal and uncommon courage. When she died at age eighty-three, she was buried 5 November 1623 in the Grenville aisle vault in St. Mary's Church. Her leadership, bravery, and wisdom had sparked the colonization of America.[48]

Grenville's Great Plan to Conquer the World was carried by word across the Atlantic Ocean to the Chesapeake Bay, up the York, the Pamunkey, and South Anna rivers to Virginia. Word passed from generation to generation, from Devonshire to settlers, "Soldiers be valiant. Remember Sir Richard Grenville and Lady Mary. Carry out their Great Plan."

Chapter 9
BESS THROCKMORTON RALEIGH
(1565 - 1647)

To avoid the confusion at the English court about two "Elizabeths," seven-year-old Elizabeth Throckmorton responded to "Bess." She was constantly reminded of the sacrifices of her parents, Ambassador Nicholas and Anne Carew Throckmorton, while they attended King Edward VI and Queen Jane Grey.[1] Her mother served as deputy for Queen Jane Grey at the christening of the son of Protestant Hot Gospeller Edward Underhill. And, her mother suffered imprisonment and mental torture at the side of ex-queen Jane Grey in the Tower of London.[2]

The ambassador's daughter inherited traits of leadership and goodwill and avoided confusion at court by using correct manners. When her father was exiled in France in the time of strife and violence, he plotted to aid Protestant forces by robbing the English treasury. When this ambassador spoke out during an intrigue in an English court, he was imprisoned, then poisoned. When Bess was in shock from this news of her father's death, courtiers surrounded her with sympathy. The child responded with a smile and curtsey.[3]

Weather permitting, this youngest maid-of-honor accompanied strong-willed Elizabeth around Greenwich Palace garden at a fast pace. Her Majesty suggested certain hedges and rose beds should be trimmed, and consulted the sundial in the front garden where all time began. Determined to maintain her security in England when commerce at sea was paramount, the queen taught Bess to wave to ships from the river's edge. The child occasionally won games in the recreation room. They played backgammon, and she encouraged her royal opponent to capture pawns at chess. With courtiers, she practiced for ballet performances by pointing her toes in front of the mirror. Although Bess danced with the royal guard until morning, she cheerfully pampered Elizabeth at six o'clock breakfasts. When ridiculous tales were amusing, Bess controlled her laughter and earned the reputation of a favorite maid-of-honor.[4]

During palace plottings, conspiracies and intrigues, some courtiers designed to separate the queen from her crown and to place prisoner Mary Queen of Scots, on the throne. After Elizabeth refused the hand of Philip of Spain, and remained unmarried, she flirted with suitor after suitor. When the Act of 1585 made it treason for a Catholic priest to be in England, the queen enjoyed the young woman's company more than remaining involved in the state affairs.[5]

Favorite maids-of-honor and three hundred gentlemen rode in Queen Elizabeth's caravan to the Earl of Hertford's party on his fabulous West Country estate. At the candlelight buffet banquet, figures of castles, tiny trumpeters, standards of heraldry and coats-of-arms of nobility were sculpted in sugar-work decorations on the cake. Bess tasted lobster and delicately sampled some of the thousand dishes before the queen enjoyed them. As the evening waned, guests relaxed under the silver canopy of state at the moon-shaped pond to enjoy elaborate fireworks.[6]

On 26 September 1580, favorite courtiers rode to Deptford harbor and ascended the boarding ramp to the quarter deck of the *Golden Hind*. Banners in gold on silk damask were decorated with fleur-de-lys, and lions were displayed on blue and red backgrounds. Her Majesty knighted Sir Frances Drake for his noble steps to bring gold and silver to England. This feat proved the current belief that cunning and daring enterprises at sea could overcome all obstacles of wealth and power. The artist Zucchero painted Queen Elizabeth holding the orb in her hand on Drake's ship that had circumnavigated the world.[7]

When traveling in the West Country to Exeter Cathedral, the splendid arches of the two great Norman towers served as their landmark. Although damaged during the Reformation, this magnificent cathedral surpassed every church of its

Chapter 9: Bess Throckmorton Raleigh

kind in England and Wales. Figures of angels, prophets, kings, and soldiers covered the Image Screen. Inside, the longest stretch of Gothic vaulting in the world--more than three hundred feet in length--gave the effect of high palm trees. High on the wall in the minstrels' gallery on the north side of the nave, figures of angels held musical instruments including the bagpipe, recorder, viol, and Jew's harp. The trumpet, hand organ, and cymbals on the interior of the cathedral charmed Bess.[8]

In Lord John Gilbert's pew, "The Mother of the Century," known as Catherine Champernown, looked upward to the vaulted ceiling to inspire her five little gentlemen with ideals of chivalry and adventure. Her fearless sons were John, Humphrey, and Adrian Gilbert, and their half-brothers Walter and Carew Raleigh. Their indoctrination of New Learning of Protestants was based upon tales of oppression. These boys were taught that no conquered nation could be ruled with gentleness. Neither were mining and raising sheep sufficient endeavors.

After Lord Gilbert's death in 1547, Catherine married Walter Raleigh the elder. His knightly emblem "W.R." was installed in handsome stained glass in the farmhouse kitchen at Hayes Barton, Devonshire. Walter Raleigh, the younger, had thick, dark hair, a bright complexion, and was full of life while collecting rocks, searching for silver, and pursuing archeological adventures.[9]

During his childhood, the family continued to gather inside the fortress-like wall of Catherine's Compton Castle. His famous mother dominated the buttery, pantry, and kitchen area and attended the well-stocked wine cellar. Spirited worship services based upon New Learning ideas were conducted weekly in the chapel. These lads practiced lessons of knightly skills and aspired to become soldiers. Their traits of pride, envy, and greed were of no consequence. During the school of war in the tilt-yard, each little soldier chose a fearless course. In challenging adventures on the saddle, the sharp edges of glistening swords and rapiers were tested. Procedures of parrying, thrusting, side-steping, and feinting became the natural gestures that inspired courage and self-confidence. The eldest son John handled the sword with pride, studied admiralty law, and learned to divide the spoils of prize ships. Humphrey, inheritor of a choleric complexion, laughed, joked and teased his brothers while fencing. Riding in the saddle like a madman, he used conversational

French, Spanish, and Portuguese. He adopted the animal spirit of the Spanish soldier, Cortez, Governor of Mexico, where enemy soldiers marching under his standard were rewarded. Well-informed about properties of tin, silver and gold, Humphrey melted down his own baby cup.[10]

Humphrey and Adrian Gilbert studied under the noted mathetician Dr. John Dee, and associated with men of ambition, and Walter Raleigh joined the Society of Antiquities. Such soldiers, navigators, and explorers in the New World depended upon the North Star for guidance.[11]

Almost immediately after Walter returned from Newfoundland in 1578, he became the prime favorite of the queen. With his cousin Sir Richard Grenville, Raleigh had pursued whaling and trapping wild animals on luckless expeditions. In 1582, upon his introduction to Bess, in the circle of maids-of-honor, she realized he was a protege of the queen's favorite Leicester.[12]

Bess read the account of Sir Humphrey Gilbert's death in 1583: "Monday, the ninth of September in the afternoon, the frigate was near cast away, oppressed by waves, yet at that time recovered; and giving forth signs of joy, the General, sitting abaft with a book in his hand, cried unto us in the *Hind* so oft as we did approach within hearing, "We are as near to heaven by sea as by land." At twelve o'clock that night the lights on his ship, the *Squirrel*, suddenly disappeared, and she was seen no more. Sir Humphrey, among others, had received the first Letters Patent granted by the crown for planning an English colony in Ireland.[13]

On February 1583-4, Letters Patent were granted Sir Adrian Gilbert and Walter Raleigh to search for the North-west Passage to Labrador and China, where dangerous sea monsters and icebergs hampered discoveries. Ill-suited to spend his life in luxury, Raleigh lost 10,000 pounds in English money in this fatal expedition. Among the favors heaped upon Raleigh in April, were two estates that included the district Virginia, to be named as she recommended in honor of the virgin queen, Elizabeth.[14]

Bess, thirteen years his junior, secretly admired Raleigh's conduct and stout heart. Dressed like a wealthy courtier, he became a top attraction at court and the center of attention. When he gallantly spread a rich cloak in the mud for the queen,

Chapter 9: Bess Throckmorton Raleigh

this maid-in-waiting surmised he carried a prince's purse. In 1584 he knelt before the queen with a twinkle in his eye to be knighted "Sir Walter Raleigh"![15]

Her Majesty awarded Raleigh numerous appointments and granted him a portion of Sir Humphrey Gilbert's patent to America. Her favorite knight received the monopolies of sweet wines and playing cards. Because of his level head, Raleigh was appointed warden of the stannaries of tin and mines of Devonshire and Cornwell, and vice-admiral of two counties. Her extravagant gifts included an Irish castle at Waterford and forty thousand acres. The territory Wyngandacoia, extending from Maine to Florida and westward to the Appalachian Mountains, was firmly renamed Virginia. According to the Oath of Supremacy, the Queen would be the supreme governor, and no foreign prince would have jurisdiction in Virginia. Selected commissioners controlled the English by jurisdiction over the church. In 1584, Puritans who wanted to renounce this Oath of Supremacy instead agreed to adopt the sign of the cross in the sacrament of Baptism. Those elected to Parliamment detected Raleigh's mocking wit.[16]

After ladies supplied necessities for Raleigh's ships in 1585, the expedition to colonize set forth under the command of his cousin Sir Richard Grenville. The hundred men who lived a year under the command of Ralph Lane on Roanoke Island returned dispirited by hardships. Another last attempt to colonize America in May 1587 was made by Raleigh.[17]

According to Exeter Guild's secret manuscript, Raleigh's voyages of discovery turned into brazen piracy. This document read, ". . .weary, (Raleigh) offered the benefit of all his discoveries in America, retaining one-fifth of the profits to our Merchant Adventurers, and was met with this rebuff. . ." The Devonshire Merchants Association showed little sympathy for Raleigh. They felt he cheated them, and they voted to invest their money for America with Adrian Gilbert and navigator John Davis.[18]

When Raleigh was appointed "Shepherd of the Seas" by Her Majesty, Bess admired his stout heart. Furious courtiers had attempted to thwart Raleigh in his fearless climb from field and council chamber to Captain of Her Guard in 1587. In order for the navy to be readily manned in times of emergency, the queen encouraged schools for seamanship in fisheries in personal waters.[19] Raleigh had the exclusive royal right to profit from fishing for cod and walrus off Newfoundland, for salmon spawning in the Blackwater River, Ireland, and for herring offshore the Channel Islands. Bess attended the queen on the *Ark Raleigh* that sailed northwestward and southwestward searching out enemy ships off Jersey and other Channel Islands. These travels aroused Her Majesty's passion for adventure.

Bess catered to the queen's efforts to minimize her age when dressing for various activities, and pantomimed exercises in the tilt yard to encourage fitness. This maid-of-honor crocheted a flattering collar and stylish ruffs to complement the jeweled necklace and green satin gown Elizabeth wore on important occasions. The queen attracted suitor after suitor.[20]

She called married maids "fools," and rarely participated in weddings. One maid who rashly married the queen's suitor was marched to prison. Early in her reign Elizabeth flirted publicly with the Earl of Leicester, considered marrying the Archduke Charles of Vienna, and encouraged Prince Eric of Sweden.[21]

Bess and courtiers in shimmering silver and white dresses bestowed lavish smiles upon the strange Duke of Anjou and his attendants at royal functions in the late 1570s and early 1580s.[22] She chatted amusingly about nothing at cockfights, rode to hunts in Hyde Park, and bent low over the bowling green. Her lips remained sealed while weeping women revealed the terrors of matrimony to the queen, who, vexed with anguish, spent a sleepless night. When Elizabeth resolved to remain unmarried, her maids-of-honor triumphed.

A scandal erupted when Raleigh's tennis ball was ruled "OUT" in the 16th century game of fives between the walls of buildings at Westminster. When this emotional player with his thick Devonshire accent disputed the umpire, he was dragged in a temper tantrum to the Tower.[23]

The ultimate downfall came to Bess when Her Majesty forbade Raleigh to meet the Spanish fleet sailing from the West Indies in 1591. The Queen ordered him to remain by her side. Bess, the favorite maid, played the lute, sang love ballads with veiled eyes and cast stealthy glances to woo Raleigh. When they

Chapter 9: Bess Throckmorton Raleigh

danced, he whispered phrases of poetry about love and promoted a secret meeting. In July 1592, when the queen thought Raleigh was loving one of her maids of honor, he was briefly committed to the Tower for offending Her Majesty.[24]

When Bess abandoned the strict criteria of behavior, her emotions betrayed her. She put off her head wreath, tucked up her clothes, and donned a large cloak like a man's for the secret meeting on the bank of the Thames. Here, Raleigh offered her a chance to draw on, and inhale, Virginia tobacco in his silver bowled pipe. They exchanged secret wedding vows.[25]

Bess and Raleigh knew the marriage laws of the Church of England required a wedding ceremony be performed by a Church of England minister and in church, if possible. Bess observed the time of day should be morning, and the time of year between special seasons in the church calendar such as Advent, Epiphany, Easter, and Pentecost. Raleigh disapproved the laws of the Church of England. Nevertheless, their marriage was binding.[26]

Bess, proven with child, was in peril of discovery. Recalling the maids imprisoned in the Tower, she feared Her Majesty would order her to the chopping block. Attempting to change her appearance with jewelry, she implored Raleigh to tell the queen of the secret wedding on the river bank. Instead, Raleigh composed and sent poetry to Elizabeth that declared his frenzied love for Her Majesty, and he vowed the queen hunted like the goddess Diana and walked like Venus.[27] Tension grew between Bess and the queen. After her own downfall, Bess shrewdly demanded justice.

Her efforts were fruitless. For rashly marrying the Queen's suitor and offending Her Majesty, Bess and Raleigh were marched to the Tower of London in July 1592. Here, they remained prisoners. Bess heard moans and groans of those tortured on the racks, and was subjected to the filth and rotten food. While Raleigh occupied himself by writing the history of the mines, Bess sang hymns and songs she learned as a child.

Years later, he wrote Bess, "I chose you and loved you in this happiest time."[28] Agreements drawn up by Raleigh's solicitor, Sir John Dodderidge, explained English common laws concerning women. These stated that before a man came to a wife with his love, it was customary for a husband to assure his wife one third of his holdings. However, "If a woman makes an elopement, the dower is forfeited."[29]

In the court of law, arrangements were made for the disposition of Raleigh's estate. These included the entailment of Sherborne Castle, a recent gift from the Queen to Raleigh, whereby Bess and her unborn child received revenues from Sherborne until her death.[30] The prison doors remained closed.

After the sinking of the *Revenge*, Raleigh, in a treatise in favor of Sir Richard Grenville, criticized Sir Thomas Howard, admiral of the English navy. When the great prize carrack *Madre de Dios* arrived in Dartmouth harbor, Her Majesty decided to release Raleigh from prison. He was sent to Dartmouth to stop the pillage of the Spanish ship. Walter appeared in a plumed hat and velvet cape. He dejectedly told his half-brother Sir John Gilbert, "I am the Queen's captive. I loved and married a maid-of-honor."[31]

After the baptismal ceremony of Walter Raleigh, Jr., on 1 November 1593, the queen relented and granted Raleigh partial freedom, but forbade the couple to come to court. When the carriage with Bess and Raleigh passed the steel gate of the Tower of London that slammed shut, they headed towards Sherborne Castle.[32] Here, Bess studied housewifery as described in *Delight for Ladies* until she became an expert in distillation and preserved fruits. She experimented with sweet powders and personal ointments until she was adept in homemaking. She remembered secrets for making sugar candy. And, she knew how to plant tobacco and Irish potatoes.

While writing a book about mines in Cornwall, Raleigh grew increasingly fascinated by the legend of Spanish wealth. He was issued a commission to plunder towns on the Spanish Main. Alarmed by the adventure, Bess wrote to Lord Burghley. She begged him to stay her husband, without furthering his hopes of an expedition.

Raleigh grudgingly remained at home during the first expedition to the Orinoco. He settled down to read the history of the Spanish Empire, until he became convinced England must destroy Spanish power in America. Since England

Chapter 9: Bess Throckmorton Raleigh

was too weak at sea to close the routes between America and Spain, he focused on the rich, beautiful empire of Guiana, and paid special attention to sailing to Trinidad.[33]

Bess knew he studied Cabot's instructions that read, "To investigate perils of the sea, and conditions under which the voyage could succeed, send ahead scouts or scout, so the company may be advised of proceedings and foresee public good. . . to provide such things (from the voyage) so the King, Lords of counsel, whole company, also your wives, children, kinfolks, elders, friends, families, be replenished in their hearts to know your enterprise."[34]

In 1595 Raleigh sailed with five ships for Trinidad, Orinoco, and the gold mining territory.[35] With little wherries constructed in haste in Trinidad, he plundered towns of the Spanish Main. The gold in the imperial city christened El Dorado exceeded any other in the world. While drawing his map of the Orinoco River in preparation of planting a colony, Raleigh and his cousin, John Grenville, survived famine, unclean water, poisoned arrows, snakes, and hard travel. The dirt carried aboard and tested in the Goldsmith's Hall, showed marquisette was in El Dorado![36]

He returned to Bess at Sherborne with pineapples, lichens, mosses, and orchids. From the natural wonderland with tropical forests, rushing rivers, exotic animals, high mountains, and Amazon women, Walter brought her presents. She fingered scarlet feathers from macaws, and blue and yellow feathers from wings of noisy birds in the rain forest. With these exotic touches and prickly stems of cactus from the New World, Bess decorated the reddish mahogany tables, and enjoyed the chairs and closets imported to Sherborne.[37]

Bess read the diary passages about the expedition intended for Her Majesty. "Guiana has more gold by manifold than the Indies or Peru; most of the kings are Her Majesty's vassals and desire English protection from the Spanish. . . When we passed any branch of a river to view land, and stayed from boats six hours, we were driven to wade to the eyes at return. (To return) was impossible because of swiftness and floating woods. In June, July, August or September, it was impossible to navigate the rivers for the fury of the current. . . Nine or ten men apiece with victuals and arms (were) about 400 miles from the ships . . . subjected to perils, diseases. All desired to serve her majesty and the Company. . . No prison in England was more unsavory."

Bess was fascinated with the description of warlike Amazon women. . ."The Queen and Amazon women were accompanied by men once a year. . .in April cast lots for valentines. They feast, dance, and drink wine until the moon is done, and depart to the province. If they conceive. . . delivered of a son, they return him to the father; if a daughter, they nourish it. . ."

Bess read on, "If we entered the land over the mountains, we should satisfy ourselves with gold. . . (There was) a nation whose heads appeared not above their shoulders. . . eyes in their shoulders, mouths in the middle of breasts, most mighty men . . . useing bows, arrows, and warlike." Raleigh concluded there was gold in every province.[38]

His final words were, "I might be king of the Indians were it but vanity. . .They fed me with fresh meat." Early in 1597 he published *The Discovery of the large, rich, and beautiful Empire of Guiana.*[39]

Although the Captain of Her Guard again rode by the Queen's side, Raleigh and Bess headed the gossip list. The couple were prominent enough at court to be consulted on matters of state. And, Raleigh seriously participated in a duel.[40] As Governor of Jersey Island from 1600 to 1603, Raleigh again had contact with the Newfoundland fishery business. The ladies Leicester, Southampton, Northumberland and Rich snubbed Bess, calling her, "The Fox's Wife" and Raleigh "The Fox." She covered her expression with a black Spanish fan."[41]

Bess delivered spirited speeches with a perfect appearance before Queen Elizabeth, and later before King James. Because she coped admirably with disastrous intrigues at court, this lady was considered by courtiers as a role model of self-expression. Ill-pleased with the queen's lack of attention, Bess left London. She preferred life at Sherborne Castle, where conversation centered about the Roanoke Island settlement and the Lost Colonists. The ageing queen scarcely noticed Bess was hostess at Sherborne. This castle, entailed for two hundred pounds a year, became a mecca for Christmas entertaining.[42]

Chapter 9: Bess Throckmorton Raleigh

Queen Elizabeth, after a rule of forty-four years and five months, died in 1603. James VI of Scotland became James I of England, monarch of two sepaate kingdoms united only by the crown. Peace minded King James was weary of persecution, of midnight outrages, robberies, of offending women and children, and arrests without warrant that were served upon the weak. His Majesty was determined to bring law and order to England.[43] Raleigh fell into disfavor, and in 1603 was accused of complicity in a plot against the king. Raleigh had supported Arabella Stuart's claim to the regal succession. Lord Thomas Howard had seized this opportunity to charge Raleigh with "high treason," and involvement in a Spanish conspiracy. Raleigh's security was threatened, and his rights to the codfish trade in Newfoundland were lost. Then, the judges in Raleigh's trial rendered the verdict "Guilty." Because of his conviction, Raleigh's sentence "to be hanged, drawn and quartered," was read.[44]

Bess suffered sleepless nights and developed dark circles under her eyes from the stress and tension involving the sentence of imprisonment. Steadying her hand, she read Raleigh's pitiful letter, "I send you all the thanks which my heart can conceive for your many travails and care taken for me. . .which have not taken effect as you wished. . .Do not hide yourself many days after my death. . .seek to help your miserable fortunes. . .Love God, and begin betimes to repose yourself on Him, and therein shall you find true and lasting riches and endless comfort. . .Teach your son also to love and fear God. . .Beg my dead body. . .and either lay it at Sherborne. . .or in the Exeter church by my father and mother."[45]

Even though Raleigh's execution was postponed, he remained in the Tower, and much of the time his wife and son visited him, and he had two servants. When he suffered from cold, Bess shared her shawl. She pulled her hood over her ears to shut out shrill screams from the torture racks. She encouraged Raleigh to dress like a gentleman in court attire while he was writing from memory his *History of the World*. One volume was published in 1614. During his experiments to condense fresh water from salt in the Tower garden, Bess developed roughened hands and ill-kept nails. When Meg, Countess of Cumberland, and other friends visited Bess in the Tower of London, they admired the model ship and were informed this was a gift from Prince Henry, Prince of Wales, who died in 1612. During the twelve years Raleigh was detained in the Bloody Tower, his rooms were furnished comfortably.[46]

Bess feared she would loose Sherborne Castle because of a clerical error of a single word discovered in the deed. She had studied *A Woman's Worth*. This book defended women against all men in the world, proving them to be more perfect, excellent and absolute in all actions than any men of "what quality so ever." Perhaps this gave her the courage to confront King James about the legal flaw making her claim invalid. At her interview with King James, Bess wore a muted satin brocade with white ruffs valued at less than five pounds to indicate she was of noble birth. Before the King, the attractive lady fell on her knees. Raising her hands to heaven, she pled with spirit, "God Almighty, punish those who wrongly expose me and my poor children to ruin and beggary."[47] Historians believe her prayer was answered.

Raleigh's friends and relatives obtained a warrant for his release from the Tower on 30 January 1616. He prepared an expedition to the Orinoco to search for a gold mine for King James. The proposed voyage might encounter high winds, storms, delay, illness, and death. Nevertheless, Bess contributed her revenue from Sherborne to furnish his fourteen vessel squadron. When Raleigh returned in 1617 he was a penniless outcast. And, Bess, wearing a hoop skirt to cover her arthritic knees, received the devastating news. Their son, Walter, was killed in an ambush while searching for a gold mine. When Raleigh attempted to escape imprisonment in the Tower by sailing on a French barge, Bess, standing on the quay, lovingly kissed her husband good-bye. However, by the King's orders, Raleigh was arrested for fighting the Spanish, and he was returned to the Tower.[48]

Since it was uncommon for a barrister to defend such a client, Raleigh, as a consequence of his 1604 conviction, was resentenced to die. For twelve years Raleigh, with Bess usually at his side, was imprisoned in the Tower of London.

Bess dressed meticulously in black serge to witness her husband's half-hour speech from the scaffold on Tower Hill, on 29 October 1618. Raleigh was beheaded in Old Palace Yard, Westminster.[49]

Determined to have part of his body left with her forever, Bess visited the

Chapter 9: Bess Throckmorton Raleigh

sheriff that night to see if the head had been retained. With perfect composure, she stated she had obtained the disposing of her husband's body. The sheriff, who was involved in the ordeal of dismembering Raleigh's head from his body, answered Bess. ". . .it is well, Bess, that thou mayest dispose of it dead, that hadst not always the disposing of it when alive." After midnight, while the sheriff slept, Bess grasped Raleigh's proud head, hugged it under her cloak, and kept it with her until she died at eighty-two.[50] Some alleged Raleigh's head was buried in St. Margaret's Church, Westminster.

Bess kept busy in her gardens at Sherborne Castle. Or, she arranged momentoes from the Orinoco, and Virginia, on furniture. She reread Walter's manuscript treatise in support of his cousin, Grenville, and she read Raleigh's speech about "tin" on file in the Society of Antiquities. Notes and clerk's records at court of Raleigh's heartbreaking trial remained. His manuscript, *Discovery of Guiana*, survived. Sir John Dodderidge, later Chief Justice of the King's Bench, attempted in vain to find a publisher for Raleigh's unpublished History of the World. When this was impossible, "J.D." signed the treatise, *Sir Walter Raleigh, the Valiant.*[51]

After the era of remarkable geographic discovery, when troubled people sought guidance from Bess, her younger son, Carew Raleigh, helped friends demand justice for all. Her dauntless courage, perfect appearance, and pursuit of knowledge gave those in prison the spirit to walk proudly and uprightly in adversity. Like Bess, they, too, put on a mantle of courage.

Chapter 10
ELEANOR WHITE DARE
(c1565 - c1607)

The First Lady in Virginia, Eleanor White Dare, was known for her courage and self-sacrifice, and for expecting a child. Her husband, Ananias Dare, and her father Governor John White, assisted her up the gangplank when the *Lion* sailed in May, 1587, from Sutton Pool, Plymouth. She yearned for the land of golden opportunities in America where she would sing and make a joyful noise to the Lord. She would praise Him and give thanks in the colony named Virginia for the virgin, Queen Elizabeth.

Governor John White's coat of arms with a silver field, a plain cross, gulls, and a roebuck, was designated by the proper authorities of the crown to suit his official position in Virginia. A more complicated personal banner included an ancient cote, the name White, and other families of his descent.[1] The Order of the Knights of St. John of Jerusalem granted White unique privileges to visit their plantations in the Caribbean Islands. He sailed with his standard, banner of arms, coat, target, sword, and helmet for protection, and he taught Eleanor the meaning of a Maltese Cross. At sunrise, standing on Plymouth quay, Eleanor and colonists sang hymns of peace.[2]

On two previous voyages to Virginia, White produced watercolor paintings of the American Indians cooking, fishing, and raising tobacco. The dress and tribal customs of Alogonquins in villages indicated a completely different life style from that of Eleanor. His detailed map of the Cape Hatteras area depicted a sea monster and several ship wrecks.[3]

On Plymouth dock, early risers listened when Psalm 46 was read from his Bible.

> "God is our refuge and strength,
> A very present help in trouble.
> Therefore we will not fear though the earth should change,
> Though the mountains shake in the heart of the sea;
> Though its waters roar and foam,
> There is a river whose streams make glad the city of God,
> The holy habitation of the Most High."

Attending this sunrise service with their husbands were Winifred Powell, Joyce Archard, Jane Jones, Jane Pierce, Rose Payne, Audrey Tappan, Elizabeth Viccars, Elizabeth Glane, Joan Warren, Alis Chapman. Traveling unattached were Emma Mermouth, Agnes Wood, and Margaret. All prayed for a better life abroad.[4]

Sir Richard, Captain-General, known to Eleanor as Mary Grenville's husband, boarded the *Lion* in half-trunk armor and red hose, his sword at his side. A ship supplied with earthenware and commodities were captained by Dorothée Stafford's relative, Edward Stafford, another by William Irish, and the fly boat was under command of Edward Spicer.[5] Bells tolled in nearby St. Andrew's Church, and spectators waved farewell.

Norman English, including Mademoiselle Horsey's ships from the Isle of Wight, reciprocated with help for the voyagers to Virginia. Since the recent victory at Malta of Christians over the heathen, the qualities of courage and self-sacrifice had become important in England, when Norman English reciprocated with help on American voyages. The Knights of St. John of Jerusalem, or Knights Hospitalers, known as the Knights of Malta, had supported Irish settlements free from toll, passage and customs.

The chief duty of the First Lady in Virginia was to assist her father, Governor John White, as stated in the laws of the corporation named, "The Governor and Assistants of the City of Raleigh"[6]

Eleanor would assume the title, "First Lady of Virginia in the City of Raleigh," according to the agreement signed by John White and approved by legal authorities.[7] At Lismore Castle in Waterford, Ireland, Grenville, John White, and Sir Walter Raleigh shared their allegiance to friends, to helping the poor, and to colonization interests. At that conference John White, and his daughter Eleanor, were chosen by Raleigh to explore Virginia in accordance with the laws drawn up for the settlement.

The navigational plan of the voyage was to sail to the West Indies for water and collect plants and livestock for the colony. The fleet would proceed up the American coast to Fort Raleigh where the fifteen men, left by Grenville in 1586 at Roanoke Island, would embark to return home. Because of piracy, there was no known proper track for sailing across the Atlantic. Fishermen followed this fleet's wake to Land's End, where waves broke furiously over the bar.

Eleanor had served as hostess at her father's plantation Kerrycurrihy, Newtown, Kilmore, Ireland. This once rich, war-ravaged territory, located near the plantations of Mary Grenville, had escheated, or reverted, to the crown because of the treason of Irishmen. Cork County was a bloody ulcer with disputed boundaries because hedge rows were trampled by English bulls, rams, and oxen. Only sickly cattle grazed in the scorched fields where horses were rounded up for light horsemen around the plantations. Eleanor struggled with overgrown brambles, rank grasses and filthy weeds.[8]

During her father's absences from Newtown, Ireland, persons hiding in the filthy bogs taunted Eleanor, and she feared she could be ambushed because her fair skin, blonde hair, and blue eyes set her apart from native Irish women. She coped with problems of workers in the silver mines on John White's land. When the bridge across the river and area at Newtown was completed and fortified, the natives appeared somewhat tamed.

However, guerilla bands of Irish Catholic boys and girls continued to pledge loyalty to Philip of Spain, rather than to the Protestant tendencies of Queen Elizabeth. Therefore, Eleanor, a generous hostess and friend, obeyed her father's instruction to keep a suitable distance from tenants and towns.[9] Survival in Irish plantations required stamina, and she practiced the exercises important for knights by fencing, swimming, shooting, and dueling with dummies. She looked forward to life on a large farm in the New World.

Eleanor White's marriage contract with a communicant, Ananias Dare, was negotiated and approved before the ceremony in St. Bride's Church, London. This followed the usual English pattern. According to custom and courtesy, before a man came with his love, he was assured a part of a wife's land. A wife was allowed one-third of his holdings. In this contract, Ananias was assured of owning his own plantation and a plot of his wife's land on the Chesapeake Bay.[10] Eleanor and Ananias Dare were also promised that their heirs in the New World would legally bear arms, or ensigns, forever. When arrangements were complete, their marriage was performed. Soon thereafter, Eleanor became pregnant.[11]

Thousands of acres in America were officially granted to John White on 7 January 1587 by Sir Walter Raleigh, recipient from Queen Elizabeth. Privileges were officially granted John White, Roger Bayley, Ananias Dare, Portuguese pilot Simon Fernandez, and nine others. In an attached document, the patentee John White's arms were first, as he was to be governor, followed by Roger Bayley, Ananias Dare, Christopher Cooper, William Fulwood, Roger Pratt, Dyonise Harvye, John Nicholls, and George Howe.[12] The city near the Chesapeake Bay was to be known as Raleigh.

On two previous voyages to Virginia, White had used the route with Ralph Lane to the West Indies and up the coast of America. On this voyage with his daughter, White planned to search for the fifteen men left by Grenville the year before. These ships were built, and manned with Bideford and Barnstaple crews, and they had been furnished by Mary Grenville's companions.

The governor's party, passengers, five returnees, and crew on the *Lion* knew the plan. The main purpose in the Virginia enterprise was to establish a base from which English ships could operate against the Spanish Indies and the treasure fleet.[13] Raleigh attracted colonists by issuing arms from the Order of the Garter.

Eleanor wondered why women's rights in the English colony abroad received little thought, and worried about provisions for the welfare of the settlers and her baby. Unanswered questions remained to be answered about the laws applicable to the rights of protection for women in Virginia. Legally, Eleanor depended upon her soldier-father and her husband, Ananias Dare, and upon family papers in a Fleet Street office.[14]   Below decks, the First Lady endured the motion of the lurching old ship, and she volunteered to labor and share burdens with others. She comforted the infirm and answered urgent questions about the necessity for soldiers to use the culverines, large guns, muskets, and pikes stored on deck to attack prize ships. The purser accounted for the powder, shot, and artillery aboard. And, Eleanor admitted being suspicious about pilot Simon Fernandez, because of his long record of piracy on the high seas and his right to own land. When joining the women assigned to look for strange ships on the horizon, she assured them of a safe voyage. Eleanor used a feather bed to lessen the roll, pitch, and toss of the sea, and converted her father's sea chest into a headboard away from the pumps. During the pounding of waves over the ship, she encouraged Ananias to help the weary crew and attend the sick and weak. The designated First Lady dined in the Governor's private cabin, on gold and silver plates, while the musician played for officers.

Everyone aboard listened to the Captain-General bellow instructions through the horn, "If any person shall fortune to die, or miscarry in the voyage, such apparel is to be kept by order of the captain."[15]

The Governor of Virginia, John White, was chosen because he had access to the secret journals of the commandery of knights about past daily experiences on the high seas near the Caribbean islands. And, he shared these with the governor's party. Names of people and every island known were recorded in the ship's log. Historical facts about commodities, customs, dispositions, sites, and names of metals in hills, mountains, streams, and rivers were included.[16]

Fernandez piloted the *Lion* towards Puerto Rico to take on water and supplies. Meg Clifford's husband had recently claimed a portion of the island because it had the reputation of being the pearl of the sea. As on the previous voyage to Puerto Rico, Grenville, with his hand on his sword, bellowed through the horn to those in the fort he built that was sheltered on two sides by woods and facing the sea and river. El Morro fortress built by Spain on five tiers of limestone, was now occupied by exiled Don Antonio of Portugal.[17]

On the planned route, the *Lion* approached Spanish forts at ports of trade in the palm-fringed West Indies Islands. Fernandez pointed his diamond-ring finger to sugar cane plantations belonging to the Knights of St. John. He also called the women's attention to the flash of machetes slashing off tips of raw sugar cane in the jungle. On the previous voyage, there were signs for parley that showed an intent to take aboard bananas, food, and casks of water, pineapple juice, and bay rum. On Mosquito Bay, the *Lion* followed the same planned route on the chart while women aboard suffered agony from vicious mosquito bites.

Columbus had officially claimed Hispaniola Island (Haiti) for Castile. Captain-General Grenville presented the governor of Hispaniola with a Bible, and they exchanged gifts at the banquet on the north side of the island, replete with orchids and conch shells. There, Grenville conducted an unheard-of feat. He emptied at a gulp his wine glass, chewed it, and swallowed the pieces. Afterwards, at the bull fight, he gleaned hints for uncovering the route to the Chesapeake Bay. On the ship, a bucket of black water hoisted to the deck was full of sparkling fish glowing with phosphorous, including barracuda, bonito, kingfish, and mackerel.[18] At midnight the thump-thump of drums from high in the mountains, and the report of voodoos under the tropic moon gave impetus for the *Lion* to sail away.

Following the route off the Florida keys on the eastern seaboard, Fernandez had skirted the fortified Spanish settlement at Fort Augustine, and avoided the territory on St. John's River where the French-English colony had suffered a cruel massacre. Eleanor and other weary women debarked at Saepello and St. Simons islands. From the *Lion*, passengers sighted the barrier islands, as the ship cautiously sailed northwards and passed Wokokan and Croatan. Off "Cape Hataroask," so-named by Grenville on the previous voyage, Eleanor used her father's map to identify pictures of shipwrecks and sea monsters.[19]

According to one diary, "The two and twentieth of July, we arrived safe at Hateroask where our ship and (flyboat) ankered." The governor went aboard, with forty of his best men, intending to pass up to Roanoke forthwith. He needed to confer with those fifteen Englishmen, which Grenville had left there the year before. Eleanor hoped to learn the state of the country, the savages, and to return to the fleet. Passing along the coast to the bay of Chesapeake, the passengers intended to make their seats and fort, according to the directions in writing, under the hand of

Chapter 10: Eleanor White Dare   *131*

Sir Walter Raleigh."[20]

    In mid-July 1587, pregnant Eleanor was afforded some sense of security by the sight of the longest stretch of sandy beach in the world, only a few miles wide in places. Tornado-like winds raged and roared, eating away the shifting land, and the procedure to drop anchor was treacherous. Wild swells in the narrow channel tossed the *Lion* aground off dangerous Cape Hatteras and waves loomed high over the deck. When the *Lion* ran aground, Fernandez prevented women from going ashore. He broke Sebastian Cabot's specific instruction, "No blasphemy of God, or swearing, or filthy tales or ungodly talk in company of any ships; nor dicing, carding, tabling, devilish games. . ." Such antics brought strife, venom, brawling, and sometimes murder, but neither seasoned seaman, nor Eleanor, dared to reprimand the pilot.[21]

    All the women were extremely irritated by Fernandez because they heard his bizarre account of an accident on a previous voyage near Cape Hatteras. According to this story, a sailor sat naked in chains over the side of the *Tiger* to wash himself, and a great white shark amputated his leg perfectly, and slithered away. The sailor was hauled aboard minus his leg.[22] Nevertheless, passengers encouraged Eleanor and credited pilot Fernandez for saving the ship on their voyage.

    On the dipsey lead in uncharted water the changeable depth measured one to three feet. A ten-stone fish claimed Marjorie's fishing pole, and porpoises surrounded their ship. At night, Eleanor was fearful of an assault by the ferocious savages who dived naked into the sea with bows and arrows. Passengers were extremely frightened.[23]

    In the shallow sea among hazardous sandbars, following John White's map, the *Lion* cautiously entered Trinity harbor. Numerous islands with wide straits promised easy access, and there were plenty of fish in the island waters, and the entire region was impossible to pass into without using a smaller boat.[24] However, that great body of water was inadequately explored, and sand from the tides was piled up in the mouth of Albermarle Sound.

    After morning prayers aboard, startling noises like those of wild beasts, or madmen, filled the air off Roanoke Island, and the Indian inhabitants raised a shuddering outcry against the English strangers. Then, Indian natives in canoes were hailed in a friendly manner and offered looking glasses, small knives, dolls and other trifles by the colonists. Impressed by the flattery, the Indian Manteo escorted the governor's party in the small boats to "Roanoac." And, he guided the governor's flyboat through stakes, piles, and floating debris to Indian villages dotting the shoreline. The strip of land approximately twelve miles wide was Roanoke Island.[25]

On 13 August 1587, the Governor was accompanied to Manteo's island, Croatan, to attend the baptism of Manteo, the first Indian in North America to be admitted to the Church of England.

"The 13. August, our Savage Manteo, by the commandment of Sir Walter Raleigh, was christened in Roanoke, and called Lord thereof, and of Dasamonqueponke, in reward for his faithful service."[26]

When Eleanor saw Roanoke town fishermen with long hair, knotted at the neck, she consulted her father's watercolors. Pearls hung from their ears, and they wore bracelets of pearls, beads and bones. Both men and women covered themselves before and behind with deerskins. A matronly woman with hair twisted into a knot, wore a six-strand necklace of small polished bones, and carried a gourd full of drinking water. The animal skins folded double under her breast hung down in front to the knees, and her bare back showed her body had punctures. A leather girdle that hung down the native's back, was drawn between the legs, and tied above the navel with tree moss, to cover private parts of her little daughter. The chief of the tribe had long hair tied at the end in a knot close to the ear, and cut at the crown, front to back like a cockscomb. A colored feather showed in the top of the crest, and a shorter one was on each side, and there were large pearls in his ear. His face and body were punctured or painted, and marks on his stomach indicated seizures of sickness. The elegant hide of a wild beast and the tail hanging down behind his buttocks, fit the chief. He held a stretched bow in one hand and an arrow in the other, and his body painted in a frightful manner with bright colors indicated the chief delighted in hunting and fishing.[27]

On 15 August 1587, the governor's party came upon a grotesque scene.

Chapter 10: Eleanor White Dare

Captain Spicer and Captain Cooke with Governor White went ashore at Hatteras, and proceeded to Fort Raleigh that Grenville had built on a previous voyage.[28] The scalps of the eighteen soldiers left to defend the fort were hanging from the palisade, and their bodies were found piled inside the shelter.[29] Visits to Indian settlements were marred by another ugly incident. At the sudden theft of Grenville's silver cup, he cut off the ear of the thief.

"Five days later, on the 18th of August 1587, Eleanor, daughter to the Governor, and wife to Ananias Dare, one of the assistants, was delivered of the daughter in Roanoke christened 'Virginia.'" On the Sunday following, the minister of the expedition christened Virginia Dare on Roanoke Island, proclaiming, "because this child was born in Virginia, she is named Virginia."[30] The birth of Virginia Dare brought on a joyful celebration among colonists because this child was named in honor of Queen Elizabeth, the virgin queen of England. Eleanor passed her daughter to the minister and to the friendly circle of colonists in the strange land. Virginia Dare was born and baptized in the Christian faith according to the rites of the English church.[31]

That summer of 1587, Eleanor and others requested Governor White to return to Bideford "for the sooner obtaining of supplies and other necessaries." Whereupon, he promised his ship would return to the colony with instant relief. When he sailed on the flyboat with the Indian called "Rawly," colonists were left with only a small store for emergencies.[32]

With the starving settlers, the First Lady made difficult decisions. She planned to move fifty miles father inland where she hoped to build a private single family dwelling away from the woods on her promised plantation. Then eighty-eight men, seventeen women, and eleven children, with two Indians, Manteo and Towaye, built "a high palisade of great trees, with curtains and flankers, very fort-like. And, a crew in search for a better harbor sailed northward from Albemarle Sound towards the Chesapeake Bay."[33]

Eleanor nursed little Virginia Dare while Ananias searched for gold mines. Although forbidden by English mores to associate with foreigners, she tarried to pay a necessary visit to Manteo's Indian wife on his island. To obtain victuals, the First

Lady refrained from provoking the Indians by disdain, laughing, and contempt, but used them with gentleness and courtesy.[34] She admired the finely-crafted earthenware vessels nearby on a pile of earth because they were easily carried, and held more than those fashioned on a turning wheel by English potters. She learned how to cope with venomous snakes, huge mosquitoes, wild beasts, and dangerous alligators. A fire burned evenly around the common pot containing a stew of fruit, meats, and fish, while the Indian women's group sat on the ground on a rush mat. They ate in moderation to avoid sickness from the grains of maize, deer meat, fish, or rabbit. Eleanor's only hope for survival of the colonists lay with friendly Indians.

In the fort, she assigned colonists to listen for the Indian battle cry, the shaking of seeds in gourds, singing, chanting and war-whoops around the great fire. Through thick bamboo briars, assignees watched Indians run from tree to tree with a bow and arrow, screaming to frighten the wolves, foxes, wild cats, black bears, and unwanted strangers. Women of Secota hung round pearls and polished bones around their necks, and covered their breasts like maidens.

Eleanor was haunted by her father's illustrations of watercolor in books in his sea chest in the camp. A grotesque painting pictured the barbarous treatment of revered Indian chiefs. One Indian conversed with devils, and murmured prayers day and night from the bed of skins of wild beasts. On the Pagan River at Werowance towards the north, groups celebrated regularly around sculptured poles with portraits of heads of veiled monks.[35]

While awaiting supplies, England was under wartime orders from the Queen. Governor White's supply ship, under instructions from Queen Elizabeth, had put back to Bideford.[36] After sunrise services on Roanoke Island, Eleanor regularly climbed the tallest sand dune to watch for ships to appear upon the horizon. She drew pictures on the white sandy beach for little Virginia. In April 1588 the sad news reached her.

Hurriedly, the Roanoke Colonists took down their houses, buried chests of goods, and at the entrance Eleanor helped carve the Maltese cross and the word "CROATOAN" on a tree. Eleanor handed Ananias one of his daughter's conch shells and helped him climb a tall pine where he carved the cross and "CRO" near the top.³⁷ Governor White's books were in his sea chest near the camp.

After assigning skiffs to colonists, Eleanor, with Virginia and Ananias, crossed Roanoke Sound and headed towards Albemarle Sound. Some followed by canoe to a path westward towards the Nottoway Indians and the mountains of Robeson County. Others sailed southward towards friendly Indians. Distraught and apprehensive, they left the palisade intact. Eleanor's hurried decision involved the safety of little Virginia Dare, as they aimed for the Croatan River and for the dangerous Dismal Swamp.

On their journey northward to the filthy Dismal Swamp, in a dugout canoe, in summer heat, Eleanor and Ananias wrapped the child in a deer skin and rabbit furs sewn with animal guts to protect her against the fluxes and fevers. They hoped to reach a suitable plantation on the Chesapeake Bay where corn, squash, and pumpkins were said to grow. At sunset, they unlashed a portable wigwam and pitched tent on a patch of firm ground. Eleanor blackened her hair with charcoal, and she taught a friendly half-wolf, half-dog how to guard Virginia Dare from wildcats and snakes. She crept from pine to pine in squirrel-skin moccasins tied to her ankles, and collected wild red berries, succulent grapes, plums, cherries, and quince apples. On moonlight nights with Ananias, she hunted 'possum, and held a bag under the animal trapped up a tree. With Virginia Dare on her back, Eleanor was hampered by briers in swamp after swamp. Ten-foot tall reeds kept off every friendly breeze from coming to refresh them, although the wind whistled among the branches of white cedars. The moist swamp ground trembled under her feet and felt like a quagmire. The First Lady was a new and different Eleanor.³⁸

She well recalled the Governor's implicit instruction about the area had been, "Do not pass further into land than able to ship." Nevertheless, Eleanor paddled the canoe in the swamp where snakes hung from cypress trees, and alligators hid behind stumps in murky water, and cougars roared on shore while huge black bears stalked their prey. Noiselessly, she cast a fishing line fashioned from sinews and baited for bass or trout, into the bogs near beaver houses. Little Virginia learned to swim underwater dog-paddle style. For the campsite dinner, the Dare family speared fish and heaped them on to a pile of twigs of beech, yellow oak, and cypress, and cooked them over a fire. Slowly, the Dare family made their way towards the Chespian tribe located on a river flowing into the Chesapeake Bay. Hiding in swampy cypress groves, they observed Indians gathering stones and looking for gold. When the natives showed no signs of hostility, Ananias joined a friendly brave for a fishing trip, and they sailed across the Chesapeake Bay. They carried a canoe on a seven-mile trail across an isthmus. Ananias was seen fishing for shad on the Pamunkey River off-shore from a residence of Chief Powhatan.

Several weeks after Ananias failed to return, an Indian brave approached Eleanor with evidences that her husband was ambushed and tortured. She recognized the strands of hair and the effects of Ananias. Cuddling Virginia, and marooned at the edge of the Chespian village, Eleanor regretted trusting the fair words of strange people. She stayed in her wigwam, pondering the circumstances concerning the death of Ananias.

Governor John White had returned to England pleading for supplies where he learned the news that this country was under invasion and the Spanish Armada was sailing to England. All ships capable of fighting were stayed. The heavily armed *Brave* and *Roe,* with fifteen planters, were provisioned with relief for colonists wintering in Virginia. However, in heavy seas, White's ship was chased from Bideford to Maderia. White staggered home at the end of May. His ship anchored between Lundy and Hartland Point near Clovelly rode the next tide, put over the bar, and landed at Bideford. Other ships had similar experiences without performing the intended voyage for relief of planters in Virginia. The settlers, and Eleanor, were irretrievably lost.[39]

On 25 August 1590, Eleanor's only hope for survival was through expressions and gestures via the grapevine of Indian couriers responsible for communication. Some theorize that on 25 August 1590, Eleanor learned the *Hopewell*, owned by Sir George Carey, Governor of the Isle of Wight, was anchored off Cape Hatteras with supplies for lost colonists. For her, there were too many swamps to cross, and the ship had arrived too late to help.[40] Transports such as the *Joseph* owned by John Dodderidge and William Darracott, carrying bag wool to the English soldiers on Hispaniola Island in 1599, continued the search for the

Chapter 10: Eleanor White Dare

lost colonists.[41] Through relays of friendly Indian couriers, Eleanor received the news that the anchor line from John White's ship had broken off Ireland, and he was forced to return. Later, Jean Derickx was spotted off Cape Hatteras, taking map measurements of the area.[42]

Governor White, upon returning to Roanoke Island, found the settlers, including Eleanor, Virginia and Ananias Dare were gone. He discovered the letters "CRO" were carved in the tall pine, and the books in his trunk were in disarray.[43]

In 1602, Raleigh's ship was identified off the Virginia shore. Other English ships traded off Kecoughtan across the Chesapeake Bay.[44] When Bartholomew Gilbert ascended the Pamunkey, inquiring for lost colonists, he was wounded within sight of his boat, and deserted by his ship, Gilbert was left in the strange land. All were searching for Eleanor and daughter Virginia.[45]

With Virginia following her through marshlands, calling wild turkeys Indian fashion and using Indian language, Eleanor discovered she had no legal rights in Virginia. Months had passed when the news was brought from London that Eleanor, not heard of in England for seven years, was declared legally dead. Ananias' natural son had inherited their estates.

An English law stated that if a husband was gone for years, a woman might marry again.[46] However, King James I of England considered it criminal for an English lady to marry beyond the seas, and a common law wife could be sent to the torture chamber in the Tower of London.

A messenger warned Eleanor not to see the white men.[47] Although she was in jeopardy during crises, Eleanor shunned would-be rescuers. In 1605, Christopher Newport and soldiers from James Fort trudged through marsh-land paths approaching Ritanoe village.[48] It was reported that Newport saw a woman resembling a lost colonist from England, and that she climbed a tree, and gave a warning whistle to a little blonde girl. And, four men in English clothes were seen as they fled up the Chowan towards a few thatched pole and frame houses at Chowanoke, near the southern shore of the Chesapeake Bay.[49]

The fates of Eleanor and her daughter, Virginia Dare, remain unknown. Some historians claim an unidentified young woman with black braids launched a canoe, steadied it, and paddled far out into the Dismal Swamp, westward towards the mountains, while an adolescent squatted among marsh grasses, indicating her preference to live as an Indian.

The saga of the First Lady of Virginia, Eleanor White Dare, and the fate of her daughter Virginia lived on for centuries. Her aggressive survival techniques encouraged acquaintances, heirs, and assignees to settle and carry on with good deeds in Norfolk County, Nottoway County, Chowan, and the Dismal Swamp.[50] Dare County, North Carolina, bears the name of this remarkable family and Virginia Dare. Centuries later, people inquire, "What happened to Virginia Dare?"

Eleanor reflected the spirit of courageous, self-sacrificing women supporters of the New World. Eleanor probably recited from memory,

> "The Lord *is* my shepherd, I shall not want.
> He maketh me to lie down in green pastures: he
> leadeth me beside the still waters.
> He restoreth my soul: he leadeth me in the paths of
> righteousness for his name's sake.
> Yea, though I walk through the valley of the shadow of
> death, I will fear no evil: for thou art with me; thy rod
> they comfort me.
> Thou preparest a table before me in the presence of mine
> enemies; thou anoitest my head with oil; my cup runneth over.
> Surely goodness and mercy shall follow me all the days of
> my life and I will dwell in the house of the Lord forever."[51]

Belief in God supplied Eleanor with courage to accept her dreadful plight, and encouraged her daughter Virginia Dare to adjust to the Great Plan for the New World.

Ten remarkable women of the Tudor Courts and their influence in founding the new world between 1530-1630 included Queen Jane Grey, Dorothée Stafford, Queen Jeanne d'Albret, Mary Queen of Scots, Mary Dudley Sidney, Mademoiselle Horsey, Meg, Countess of Cumberland, Mary St. Leger Grenville, Bess Throckmorton Raleigh and Eleanor White Dare, the First Lady of Virginia.

Epilogue

Fremington pottery, a symbol of these Ten Remarkable Women of the Tudor Courts, was transported to Virginia. On 20 November 1606, the Royal Company for Virginia granted the Virginia Company permission to establish a permanent English settlement in America on land that extended northward, southward and westward. This advowson, awarded by King James I of England in 1607, included the Fishmongers Company, Exeter merchants, and the Earl of Hereford.

Shreds of utility earthenware tempered with gravel from Fremington are among the artifacts left by settlers at Jamestown. The excavation discoveries of seventeenth century of North Devon pottery at Jamestown, Yorktown, and Bermuda Hundred were hailed by archaeologists as remarkable. North Devon pottery was located under a long, narrow row house situated on a low ridge in the northeast part of New Town, parallel to the James River shore line and to the south. Unearthed in a well was a handled chafing dish made in North Devon, and in another structure was found a three-legged-pot with a stem handle at the bottom. Coarse-tempered utility earthenware from North Devon was strongly represented in the foundation ruins of a mansion.

The obsolete and ugly earthenware fired with red clay from Fremington parish and transported to Jamestown, Virginia, to Lewes, Maryland, and to Plymouth, Massachusetts became a valuable historic item. Shreds of special pottery produced before 1780 account for the centuries of on-going relationships between Bideford and Barnstaple and colonists in America.

Endnotes

1 Queen Jane Grey

1. Chalmers, *The Works of English Poets*, 1810, p. 102.

2. *Ibid.*

3. Hester W. Chapman, *Lady Jane Grey*, 1962, p. 52, p. 55, p. 57.

4. A. F. Scott, *The Tudor Age,* 1975, p. 82.

5. H. W. Chapman, *Lady Jane Grey*, 1962, p. 45, p. 48, p. 80, pp. 29-33.

6. H. W. Chapman, *Lady Jane Grey*, 1962, pp. 29-33.

7. H. W. Chapman, *Lady Jane*, 1962, p. 45, p. 80.

8. H. W. Chapman. *Lady Jane*, 1962, p. 53.

9. H. W. Chapman, *Lady Jane*, 1962, p. 23, pp. 29-34.

10. Samuel Hopkins, *The Puritans and Queen Elizabeth*, n. d., Vol. I, p. 53; H.W. Chapman, *Lady Jane*, 1962, p. 46.

11. J. D., *The Laws, Resolutions, or the Lawes Provision for Women, or Women's Rights*, 1632, n.p.

12. H. W. Chapman, *Lady Jane*, 1962, p. 82.

13. *DNB*, s. v. Sir John Dudley, s. v. Lady Jane Dudley, 1917.

14. *NSE*, s.v. Sir John Dudley, 1931.

15. C. H. Garrett, *The Marian Exiles*, 1938, #112, #357, #366; J. G. Nicholas, *The Chronicle of Queen Jane*, 1750, pp. 2-7.

16. H. W. Chapman, *Lady Jane*, 1962, pp. 90-97.

17. H. W. Chapman, *Lady Jane*, 1962, p. 76., p. 82.

18. *Ibid.*

19. Chalmers, *The Works in English Poets*, 1810, p. 101.

20. H. W. Chapman, *Lady Jane*, 1962, p. 82.

21. H. W. Chapman, *Lady Jane*, 1965, p. 111.

22. H. W. Chapman, *Lady Jane*, 1962, p. 122.

23. J. G. Nicholas, *The Chronicle of Queen Jane*, 1750, pp. 2-7.

24. Harris Nicholas, *The Literary Remains of Lady Jane*, 1825, pp. cxvii-cxliii; H. W.Chapman, *Lady Jane*, p.102.

25. *DNB*, s. v. Lady Jane Grey, 1917; H. W. Chapman, *Lady Jane*, 1962, p. 102.

26. Christian Gasgoine, *The Castles of Great Britain*, 1980, p. 14.

27. *DNB*, s. v. Sir John Dudley, 1917.

28. *DNB*, s. v. Sir John Dudley,, 1917; H. W. Chapman, *Lady Jane*, 1965, p. 107.

29. Chalmers, *The Works of English Poets*, 1810, p. 102.

30. H. W. Chapman, *Lady Jane*, 1965, pp. 47, 48, 200.

31. H. W. Chapman, *Lady Jane*, 1965, pp. 169-171.

32. *DNB*, s.v. Lady Jane Dudley; H. W.Chapman, *Lady Jane*, 1965, pp. 177-178.

33. N. H. Nicholas, *The Historic Peerage of England*, 1857, pp. 47, 48.

34. N. H. Nicholas, *The Historic Peerage of England*, 1857, pp. 41-44.

35. N. H. Nicholas, *The Historic Peerage of England*, 1857, p. cii.

36. N. H. Nicholas, *The Historic Peerage of England*, 1857, p. 53.

2 Dorothée Stafford

1. *DNB*, s.v. Sir William Stafford.

2. *Ibid.*

3. C. Gascoigne, *Castles of Britain*, 1975, p. 86.

4. *Ibid.*

5. *Leeds Castle, Illustrated History and Guide,* 1985, pp. 1-27.

6. G. H. Chettle, *Hampton Court Palace*, 1975, pp.1-14.

7. *Ibid.*

8. Paul Henry, *Life and Times of John Calvin*, 1583, p. 323.

Endnotes

9. C. H. Garrett, *The Marian Exiles*, 1938, p. 16, 16n.

10. C. H. Garrett, *The Marian Exiles*, 1938, p. 11.

11. C. H.Garrett, *The Marian Exiles*, 1938, p.11; J. A. Froude, *The English in the West Indies*, 1860-93, 1900, p. 455.

12. Charles Martin, *Les Protestants Anglais Réfuies à Genèva au Temps de Calvin 1555-1560*, 1915, pp. 331-337.

13. C. H. Garrett, *The Marian Exiles*, 1938, p. 16, 16n.

14. Charles Martin, *Les Protestants Anglais*, 1915, pp. 331-337.

15. S. A. Laval, *History of Reference in France*, 1738, p. 147.

16. Paul Henry, *Life and Times of John Calvin*, 1853, Vol. III, p.323.

17. Samuel R. Gardiner, *A Students History of England*, 1904, p. 430.

18. John S. C.Abbott, *Makers of History*, 1942, p. 11.

19. Charles Martin, *Les Protestants Anglais*, 1915, p. 332.

20. *Edinburgh Review*, "...troubles at Frankfort," Vol. 85, pp. 398-426.

21. William Blackburn, *Admiral Coligny and the Rise of the Huguenots*, n.d., pp. 75-77.

22. *Ibid.*

23. *Ibid.*

24. *The Hymnbook*, 1945, p. 144.

25. *Johns Hopkins Studies*, "French Protestentism," 1918, Vol. 36.

26. *DNB*, s.v. Sir Francis Knollys.

27. Paul Henry, *Life and Times of John Calvin*, 1853, p. 323.

28. Charles Martin, *Les Protestants Anglais*, 1915, p. 333, p. 352.

29. *Ibid.*

30. Porter Mignet, *A History of Mary Queen of Scots*, 1863, p. 40, p. 67.

31. William Blackburn, *Admiral Coligny and the Rise of the Huguenots*, n.d., pp. 75-77.

32. *Ibid.*

33. *The Hymnbook*, 1945, p. 144.

34. Charles Martin, *Les Protestants Anglais*, (1915) pp. 331-337.

35. *WestminsterShorter Catechism*, pp. 2, 3.

36. *The Hymnbook*, 1945, p. 24.

37. Paul Henry, *Life and Times of John Calvin*, 1853, Vol. II, p. 323.

38. John S. C. Abbott, *Makers of History*, 1942, p. 11.

39. Samuel Hopkins, *The Puritans*, n.d., Vol. I, p. 141.

40. G. B. Parks, *Richard Hakluiyt*, 1949, 3rd series, Vol. VI, p. 410.

41. G. B. Parks, *Richard Hakluyt*, 1949, 3rd series, Vol. VI, p. 410; Warner F. Gookin, "Who was Bartholomew Gosnold?" *William and Mary Quarterly*, 1949, 3rd series, Vol.VI, p. 399, pp. 412-413.

42. Paul Henry, *Life and Times of John Calvin*, 1853, Vol. I, pp. 374-375.

43. Paul Henry, *Life and Times of John Calvin*, 1853, Vol. I, pp. 374-375.

3 Queen Jeanne d'Albret

1. Robert Ritter, *Le Pay de Bearn*, 1924, introduction, photographs; Lord Russell of Liverpool, *Henry of Navarre and the Huguenots*, 1961, p.12, p. 196.

2. Porter Mignet, *A History of Mary Queen of Scots*, 1863, p. 52, p. 61; Julian Coudy, *The Huguenot Wars*, 1969, ff. 287, n. chart; Paul Henry, *Life and Times of John Calvin*, 1853, Vol. II, pp. 87, p. 88.

3. S. R. Gardiner, *A Students History of England*, 1904, p. 430; S. A. Laval, *History of Reference in France*, 1727, p. 147; F. C. Palm, *Calvinism and the Religious Wars*, 1932, p. 30.

4. Field trip Lescar Cave, 1987.

5. See Note 1.

6. R. Ritter 1966 photograph: R. J. Travis, *The Travis Family*, 1954, p. 83; *Nobilaire et Amoral de Bretagne,* Vol. III, p. 323; *Dictionaire Heraldique de Bretagne,* MDCCCXCV, p. 64; P. S. Ormond, *Basques and their Country*, 1926, p. 19, pp. 133-134.

7. P. S. Ormond, *Basques*, 1926, p. 24.

8. Lord Russell, *Henry of Navarre*, 1969, p. 44; John E. H. Nolan "Life in the Land of Basques," *National Geographic*, February 1964, p. 147ff.

9. F. Willert, *Henry of Navarre*, 1893 p. 45; Lord Russell, *Henry of Navarre*, 1969, p. 20, p. 21, p. 196.

10. R. Ritter, *Le Pay de Bearn*, 1966, Introduction; Field trip Lescar Cave, 1987; J. E. H. Nolan, *National Geographic*, February 1954, p. 159-174.

11. R. Ritter, *Le Pays*, 1966, p. l.

Endnotes 145

12. Paul Henry, *Life of John Calvin*, 1853, Vol. II, pp. 87, 88; W. H. Ireland, *Memories of Henry the Great*, 1824, Vol. I, p. 32.

13. P. S. Ormond, *Basques*, 1926, p. 45, pp. 47-48; R. Ritter, *Le Pay*, 1966, Introduction.

14. P.S. Ormond, *Basques*, 1926, p. 58; P. E. S. Nolan, *National Geographic*, February 1954, pp. 159-174.

15. Oswyn Murray Collection Wills 3/36, June 7, 1554, Apr. 1566; *Lists and Analysts Foreign State Papers,* F118 No. 464, pp. 293-294.

16. C. Garrett, *Marian Exiles*, 1838, p. 17; S. B. Weeks, *The Lost Colony*, p. 109.

17. Henry M. Baird, *History of the Huguenots in France*, 1879, Vol. II, p. 81.

18. A. Fraser, *Mary Queen of Scots*, pp. 71-73.

19. Lord Russell, *Henry of Navarre*, 1969, p. 27; P. F. Willert, *Henry of Navarre*, 1893, p. 22; S. A. Laval, *Hist. of Ref.in France*, 1737, p. 147.

20. Lord Russell, *Henry of Navarre*, 1969, p. 197.

21. P. S. Ormond, *Basques*, 1926, p. 16; Lord Russell, *Henry of Navarre*, 1969, pp. 196-97; J. Coudy, *The Huguenot War*, 1969, p. 143.

22. P. F. Willert, *Henry of Navarre*, 1893, p. 53n.; H. M. Baird, *History of the Huguenots in France, 1875-93*, 1879, Vol. II, p. 52.

23. W. Blackburn, *Admiral Coligny*, n.d., pp. 75-77; C. Martin, *Les Protestants*, 1915, pp. 331-337; G. Bancroft, *History of the United States*, 1845, Vol. I, p. 64; C. H. Garrett, *Marian Exiles*, 1938, p. 17.

24. Lord Russell, *Henry of Navarre*, 1969, p. 197; S. Hopkins, *The Puritans*, 1875, Vol. II, p. 329; C. W. Baird, *History of Huguenots*, 1879, Vol. II, p. 141, pp. 150-151.

25. W. H. Ireland, *Memories of Henry the Great*, 1824, Vol. I, p. 40; S. A. Laval, *History of Reference*, 1737, p. 147; P. S. Ormond, *Basques*, 1926, p. 31.

26. P.S. Ormond, *Basques*, 1926, p. 71; Field trip, 1976.

27. C. G. Kelly, *French Protestantism*, Vol. 36, p. 17.

28. H. M. Baird, *History of Huguenots 1875-93*, 1879, Vol. II, p. 350; Lord Russell, *Henry of Navarre*, 1961, p. 76.

29. H. M. Baird, *Hist of Huguenots*, 1879, Vol. II, p. 52.

30. S. A. Laval, *History of Reference*, 1737, p. 147; H. M. Baird, *History of Huguenots*, 1879 II, p.303.

31. W. H. Ireland, *Memories of Henry the Great*, 1824, Vol.I, p. 40; J. Coudy, *The History of Huguenot Wars*, 1969, p. 22ff.

32. W. H. Ireland, *Memories of Henry the Great*, 1824, Chapter I; H. M. Baird, *Hist of Huguenots*, 1879, Vol. II, p. 52; L. Russell, *Henry of Navarre*, 1969, p. 34.

33. J. S. C. Abbot, *Makers of History*, 1942, p. 11.

34. H. M. Baird, *History of Huguenots 1879-83*, 1879, Vol. II, p. 374.

35. C. G. Kelly, *French Protestantism*, Vol. 36, p. 17.

36. H. M. Baird, *History of Huguenots*, 1879, Vol II, p. 519; L. Russell, *Henry of Navarre*, 1969, p. 197; Robert Ritter, *Le Pay de Bearn*, 1966, photo d'Arricau-Bordes.

37. C. G. Kelly, *French Protestantism*, Vol. 36, p. 17; C. Martin, *Les Protestants Anglais*, 1915, pp. 331-337.

38. H. M. Baird, *History of Huguenots*, 1879, Vol. II, p. 405.

39. J. Coudy, *The Huguenot Wars*, 1969, p. 46.

40. H. M. Baird, *History of Huguenots*, 1879, Vol. II, p.405.

41. J. Coudy, *The Huguenot Wars*, 1969, p. 46; H. M. Baird, *History of Huguenots*, 1879, Vol. II, p. 405.

42. C. Read, *Secretary Walsingham*, 1925, Vol. I, pp. 1-3.

43. *The Maritime Siege of Malta 1565*, n. d., p. 30, p. 31; E. King and H. Luke, *Knights of St. John*, 1967, p. 141.

44. H. N. Baird, *History of Huguenots*, 1879, Vol. II. pp. 519-521; R. Ritter, *Le Pay de Bearn*, 1966, p. 1.

4 Mary Queen of Scots

1. Antonia Fraser, *Mary Queen of Scots*, 1969, p. 44, p 49. David Hay Fleming, *Mary Queen of Scots*, MDCCXCVIII, p. 21, notes.

2. Julian Coudy, ed. *The Huguenot Wars*, 1969, ff. 287; Paul Henry, *Life and Times of John Calvin*, 1853, Vol. II, pp. 87, 88; D. H. Fleming, MDCCXCVIII, pp. 225, 241.

3. A. Lang, *Mystery of Mary Stuart*, 1902, pp. 22, 36.

4. D. H. Fleming, *Mary Queen of Scots,* MDCCXCVIII, pp. 45, 47, 53, 257.

5. *Scottish Confession of Faith*, n. d.

6. A. Lang, *Mystery of Mary Stewart*, pp. 4, 8, 9, 15, 17, 23, 44 56; D. H. Fleming, *Mary Queen of Scots*, MDCCXCVIII, p. 300.

7. A. Lang, *Mystery of Mary Stuart*, 1902, pp. 4, 43, 44.

8. D. H. Fleming, *Mary Queen of Scots*, MDCCCXCVIII, p. 60.

Endnotes

9. D. H. Fleming, *Mary Queen of Scots*, MDCCXCVIII, p. 65, 66.

10. A. Lang, *Mystery of Mary Stuart*, 1902, p.22, 36.

11. D. H. Fleming, *Mary Queen of Scots*, MDCCXCVIII, pp. 74, 81.

12. Gordon Donaldson, *The First Trial of Mary Queen of Scots*, 1969, p. 33.

13. D. H. Fleming, *Mary Queen of Scots*, MDCCXCVIII, pp. 65, 89, 92, 93, 315.

14. D. H. Fleming, *Mary Queen of Scots*, MDCCXCVIII, pp. 104, 105.

15. Eric Linkletter, *The Royal House*, 1970, pp. 51, 89; Lord Russell of Liverpool, *Henry of Navarre and the Huguenots*, 1961, p.76; D. H.Fleming, *Mary Queen of Scots*, MDCCXCVIII. p. 103.

16. A. Lang, *Mystery of Mary Stewart*, 1902, pp. 15, 17, 56.

17. A. Lang, *Mystery of Mary Stewart*, 1902, pp. 13, 57-60.

18. *Ibid.*

19. A. Fraser, *Mary Queen of Scots*, 1969, pp. 249-58; A. Lang, *Mystery of Mary Stewart*, pp. 68-69.

20. G. Donaldson, *The First Trial*, 1969, p. 41; D. H. Fleming, *Mary Queen of Scots*, MDCCXCVIII, p. 128.

21. A. Lang, *Mystery of Mary Stewart*, 1902, p. 69; A Fraser, *Mary Queen of Scots*, 1969, p. 323.

22. A. Fraser, *Mary Queen of Scots*, 1969, pp. 31-32; A. Lang, *Mystery of Mary Stewart*, 1902, p. 4, pp. 64-70.

23. D. H. Fleming, *Mary Queen of Scots*, MDCCXCVIII, p. 408.

24. A. Lang, *Mystery of Mary Stewart*, 1902, p. xiii, pp. 3, 100.

25. A. Lang, *Mystery of Mary Stewart,* 1902, pp. 2-3, p. 102.

26. A. Lang, *Mystery of Mary Stewart*, pp. 80-84, pp. 94-95; D. H. Fleming, *Mary Queen of Scots*, p. 154.

27. Stephen Able Laval, *History of Reference in France*, 1737, p. 147; Conyers Read, *Mr. Secretary Walsingham and the Policy of Queen Elizabeth*, 1925, I pp. 1-3.

28. A. Lang, *Mystery of Mary Stewart*, 1902, p. 108.

29. A. Lang, *Mystery of Mary Stewart*, 1902, p. 135.

30. A. Lang, *Mystery of Mary Stewart*, 1902, pp 138-142.

31. A. Lang, *Mystery of Mary Stewart*, 1902, pp. 133-134, 143-144.

32. *Ibid.*

33. A. Lang, *Mystery of Mary Stewart*, 1902, pp. 179-180.

34. D. H. Fleming, *Mary Queen of Scots*, MDCCXCVIII, p. 257.

35. A. Lang, *Mystery of Mary Stewart*, 1902, p. 194.

36. A. Lang, *Mystery of Mary Stewart*, 1902, p. 186.

37. A. Lang, *Mystery of Mary Stewart*, 1902, pp. 186, 194.

38. A. Lang, *Mystery of Mary Stewart*, 1902, p. 195.

39. A. Lang, *Mystery of Mary Stewart*, 1902, pp. 204-205.

40. A. Lang, *Mystery of Mary Stewart*, 1902, p. 5, p. 205, note.

41. A. Fraser, *Mary Queen of Scots*, 1969, pp. 334ff.; A. Lang, *Mystery of Mary Stewart*, 1902, pp. 207.

42. A. Fraser, *Mary Queen of Scots*, 1969, p. 364ff; A. Lang, *Mystery of Mary Stewart*, 1902, p. 183.

43. A. Lang, *Mystery of Mary Stewart*, 1902, p. 195, pp. 378-379.

44. A. Lang, *Mystery of Mary Stewart*, 1902, p. 3.

45. A. Lang, *Mystery of Mary Stewart*, 1902, pp. 3-4.

46. A. Fraser, *Mary Queen of Scots*, 1969, p. 391; A . Lang, *Mystery of Mary Stewart*, 1902, p. 242, p. 243.

47. A. Fraser, *Mary Queen of Scots*, 1969, pp. 5, 6. *Lists and Analysis Foreign State Papers*, F118, No: 464.

48. A. Lang, *Mystery of Mary Stewart*, 1902, p. 225, p. 235.

49. A. Fraser, *Mary Queen of Scots*, 1969, pp. 442, 443.

50. A. Lang, *Mystery of Mary Stewart*, 1902, pp. 264-266.

51. A. Fraser, *Mary Queen of Scots*, 1969, p. 389. A. Lang, *Mystery of Mary Stewart*, 1902, pp. 262-282.

52. G. Donaldson, *The First Trial*, 1969, p. 92.

53. A. Lang, *Mystery of Mary Stewart*, 1902, 361-363; G. Donaldson, *The First Trial*, 1969, p. 78.

5 *Mary Dudley Sidney, Countess of Pembroke*

1. *DNB*, s. v. John Dudley, s. v. Sir Henry Sidney, 1917.

2. E. G. R. Taylor, *Tudor Geography*, 1930, pp. 76-90. *The Tower of London*, 1974, p. 45.

Endnotes

3. *DNB*, s. v. Sir Henry Sidney, 1917; *HMC,* Report on Manuscripts of L'Isle and Dudley, 1925, Vol. I, p. 15.

4. E. King and H. Luke, *Knights of St. John*, 1967, pp. 81-84.

5. E. G. R. Taylor, *Tudor Geography*, 1930 pp. 76-90.

6. *DNB*, s. v. Sir Henry Sidney, 1917.

7. *DNB*, s.v. Sir Henry Sidney.

8. H. W. Chapman, *Lady Jane Grey*, 1962, p. 102; *DNB* s. v. Sir Henry Sidney.

9. *Ibid.*

10. *DNB*, s. v. Sir Henry Sidney, 1917.

11. *HMC,* Report on Manuscripts of L'Isle and Dudley, 1925, Vol. I, p. 272.

12. Scott, Walter, *Kenilworth,* (n.d.) pp. 22, 23.

13. S. Hopkins, *The Puritans and Queen Elizabeth*, 1865, Vol. I, p. 246.

14. C. Gascoigne, *Castles of Britain*, 1980 p. 88; *The Tower of London*, 1974, p. 36.

15. See Note 5.

16. *HMC,* Report on the Manuscripts of L'Isle and Dudley, 1525, Vol. I, p. 260.

17. *Ibid.*

18. *HMC,* Report on the Manuscripts of L'Isle and Dudley, 1925, Vol. I, p. 258, p. 260.

19. *HMC,* Report on the Manuscripts of L'Isle and Dudley, 1925, Vol. I, pp. 257, 264, 380.

20. J. Derricke, "Image of Ireland", *Somers Tracts,* Collector Walter Scott, Esq., 1809, translation: Film S-8, Reel 922; P & R No: 6734, Pub. 1582, U. Va.

21. J. Derricke, "Image of Ireland", *Somers Tracts,* Collector Walter Scott, Esq., 1809, 1809, pp. 492-493.

22. P. Addleshaw, *The Cathedral Church of Exeter*, 1909, p. 20.

23. *DNB*, s.v. Sir Henry Sidney, 1917.

24. Lord Brook, *Life of Philip Sidney*, 1816, p. 61; *DNB*, s. v. Sir Henry Sidney.

25. C. Gascoigne, *Castles of Great Britain*, 1980, p. 96; *HMC,* Report on the Manuscripts of L'Isle and Dudley, 1925, p. 260.

26. *HMC,* Report on the Manuscripts of L'Isle and Dudley, 1925, p. 260.

27. *DNB*, s. v. Sir Henry Sidney, 1911; John Morley, *English Man of Letters, Sidney*, 1906, p. 179.

28. *DNB*, s. v. Sir Philip Sidney.

29. J. Morley, *English Man of Letters*, Sidney, 1906, p. 109.

30. *Ibid*.

31. J. Morley, *English Man of Letters*, Sidney, 1906, p. 176.

32. J. Morley, *English Man of Letters*, Sidney, 1906, pp. 108, 109; H. R. Fox Bourne, *Sir Philip Sidney*, 1892, pp. 3-5.

33. Theodore de Bry, *Arts in Virginia,* Spring 1973, pp.2, 3.

34. J. Derrick, "Image of Ireland," *Somers Tracts*, Collector Walter Scott, Esq., 2nd ed. 1613; Film S8, Reel 922: P. & R. No. 6734, 1582.

35. *DNB*, s. v. Sir Henry Sidney, 1911.

6 Mademoiselle Horsey

1. C. H. Garrett, *The Marian Exiles*, 1938, pp. 331-337; *DNB*, s. v. Sir Edward Horsey, 1917.

2. Field trip Normandy 1987.

3. Field trip Chateaux country 1974.

4. *Ibid*.

5. *DNB*, s.v. Sir Edward Horsey, 1917.

6. C. H. Garrett, *The Marian Exiles*, 1938, pp. 331-337.

7. *Lists and Analysis Foreign State Papers, Elizabeth I,* Vol. II, July 1590-May 1591, 1969, F118 No: 464, pp. 273, 274.

8. J. D. (Sir John Dodderidge), *Tracts*, 1630.

9. See note 5.

10. *DNB*, s. v. Sir Nicholas Throckmorton, 1917.

11. William Blackburn, *Admiral Coligny and the Rise of Huguenots*, n.d., pp. 75-77.

12. *Ibid*.

13. William Berry, *The History of Guernsey*, 1816, pp. 198-201.

14 *HMC,* Duke of Rutland, 1905, Vol. IV.

15. See Note 5.

Endnotes

16. Charles W. Baird, *History of Huguenot Immigration to America*, 1966, Vol.I, p. 60; Theodore de Bry, Arts in Virginia, Spring, 1973, p. 2, 3; C. Malcolm Watkins, *North Devon Pottery and its export to America in the 17th Century*, Smithsonian Institution Bulletin 225, 1960, p.58.

17. Charles W. Baird, *Hist of Hug Immigration to Am* 1966 Vol. I, pp. 59-62.

18. See Note 11.

19. J. Albin, *History of the Isle of Wight*, 1975, p. 192.

20. *DNB*, s. v. Sir Edward Horsey, 1917.

21. *Ibid.*

22. *Ibid.*

23. *Ibid.*

24. *Ibid.*

25. *Ibid.*

26. *Ibid.*

27. *Ibid.*

28. Julian Coudy, ed., *The Huguenot Wars*, 1969, pp. 176-179; Charles Franklin Palm, *Calvinism and the Religious Wars*, 1932, pp. 50-51.

29. J. Coudy, ed., *The Huguenot Wars*, 1969, p. 46; Alexander Dumas, *Three Musketeers*, 1906, p. 311; Lord Russell of Liverpool, *Henry of Navarre and the Huguenots*, 1961, p. 40; P. S. Ormond, *Basques and their Country*, 1926, p. 104, p. 105.

30. Lord Russell of Liverpool, *Henry of Navarre and the Huguenots*, 1961, p. 35. Henry M. Baird, *History of the Rise of Huguenots*, 1897, Vol. II, p. 427ff.

31. P. F. Willert, *Henry of Navarre and the Huguenots*, 1893, p. 69, p. 70.

32. P. F. Willert, *Henry of Navarre and the Huguenots*, 1893, p. 79 ff.

33. *Ibid.*

34. Henry M. Baird, *History of the Rise of the Huguenots*, 1897, Vol. II, pp. 457-459.

35. *Ibid.*

36. Henry M. Baird, *Rise of the Huguenots*, 1897, Vol. II, pp. 519 ff; Charles W. Baird, *History of Huguenot Emigration to America*, 1966, Vol. I, p. 149.

37. H. M Baird, *Rise of the Huguenots*, 1897, Vol. II, pp. 519ff..

38. *Ibid.*

39. Walter Scott, *Kenilworth, Leicesters's Commonwealth*, n.d., p. 22, p. 26; *DNB* s. v. Sir Robert Dudley, 1917.

40. *DNB*, s. v. , Sir Edward Horsey.

41. *Ibid.*

42. *Ibid.*

7 *Margaret Russell Clifford*

1. C. H. Garrett, *The Marian Exiles*, 1938, #357.

2. P. Addleshaw, *The Cathedral Church of Exeter*, 1899, p. 57.

3. W. T. MacCaffrey, *Exeter 1540-1640*, 1958; Field trip 1976.

4. T. Risdon, *The Chronology and Description or Survey of Exeter*, 1714, p. 328.

5. G. G. Bushnell, *Sir Richard Grenville*, 1936, p. 108.

6. R. Isacke, *Remarkable Antiquities of the City of Exeter*, 1724; Cotton Manuscript 52786, v-viii; W.T. MacCaffrey, *Exeter 1540-1560*, 1959, p. 214.

7. Andrew L. Simon, *The Noble Grapes and Great Wines of France*, 1947, p. 4.

8. E. G. R. Taylor, *The Missing Draft of Drake's Voyage*, Geographical Journal, January 1930, LXXV, No.1; Field trips St. Thomas and San Blas Islands.

9. A. N. Worth, *A History of Devonshire*, 1893, p. 18.

10. Lady Anne Clifford, *Diary of Lady Anne Clifford*, 1923, p. x; *DNB* s. v. Sir Francis Russell, 1917.

11. *Ibid.*

12. C. Gascoigne, *Castles of Britain*, 1980, p. 112.

13. *Ibid.*

14. A. Clifford, *Diary*, 1923, p. xii.

15. *Ibid*, frontpiece.

16. *DNB*, John Davis, 1917; Field trip to Lebrador, by Winston Wheeler, 1999.

17. *DNB,* s.v. George Clifford, 1917.

18. A. Clifford, *Diary*, 1923, p. 5.

Endnotes

19. *High Court of Admiralty 13/30,* 10 June 1592.

20. A. Clifford, *Diary*, 1923, p. ix.

21. A. Clifford, *Diary*, 1923, p. xiii.

22. *DNB,* s. v. Sir George Clifford, 1917.

23. A. Clifford, *Diary*, 1923, p. xviii.

24. *DNB,* s. v. Sir George Clifford, 1917.

25. *Diary of Dr. Dee*, n. d., p. 47.

26. A. Clifford, *Diary*, 1923, p. xxxiii.

27. Paul Henry, *Life and Times of John Calvin*, 1853, Vol. I, p. 374.

28. A. Clifford, *Diary*, 1923, p. xxviii.

29. *DNB,* s. v. Sir George Clifford, 1917.

30. A. Clifford, *Diary*, 1923, p. xv.

31. A. Clifford, *Diary*, 1923, p. 500.

32. A. Clifford, *Diary*, 1923, p. xxx, p. 5.

33. A. Clifford, *Diary*, 1923, pp. 5-6.

34. A. Clifford, *Diary*, 1923, pp. 7-9.

35. A. Clifford, *Diary*, 1923, p. 10.

36. A. Clifford, *Diary*, 1923, p. xxiii.

37. A. Clifford, *Diary*, 1923, p. 12, p. 13.

38. See Note 35.

39. See Note 37.

40. A. Clifford, *Diary,* 1923, p. xxiii.

41. A. Clifford, 1923, p. xvxix.

42. A. Clifford, *Diary*, 1923, p. xxviii, note.

43. *DNB,* s.v. Lady Anne Clifford; A. Clifford, *Diary*, 1923, p. xxxii.

44. A. Clifford, *Diary*, 1923, p. xxxii.

45. A. Clifford, *Diary*, 1923, pp. xlvi, xlix.

46. A. Clifford, *Diary*, 1923, p. 30.

47. A. Clifford, *Diary*, 1923, p. 37.

48. A. Clifford, *Diary*, 1923, p. xlii.

8 Mary St. Leger Grenville

1. George H. Bushnell, *Sir Richard Grenville*, 1936, pp. 52-55.

2. Major Ascott, *Bideford Parish Church*, 1950, p. 8; A. L. Rowse, *Sir Richard Grenville of the Revenge*, 1937, p. 38.

3. M. Ascott, *Bideford Parish Church*, 1950, p. 11.

4. Field Trip to Bideford, 1975; A. L. Rowse, *Sir Rich Gren*, 1937, p. 15.

5. R. Manhart, *English Commerce and Exploration in the Reign of Elizabeth*, 1927. p. 8; J. G. Kohl, *Collections of Maine Historical Society*, 1869, 2nd series, Vol. I, pp. 183-205.

6. See Note 2; Field Trip to Bideford 1975.

7. J. D. (Attributed by Thomas Wentworth to Sir John Dodderidge), 1632.

8. G. H. Bushnell, *Sir Richard Grenville*, 1936, p. 37.

9. C. Kingsley, *Westward Ho, or the Adventures of Amias Leigh*, 1911, p.22, p. 23.

10. *DNB*, s. v. Sir Richard Grenville, 1917.

11. G. H. Bushnell, *Sir Rich Gren*, 1936, pp. 214-219; R. Granville, *The History of Bideford*, 1883, p. 21.

12. Derricke, John, "Image of Ireland" *in Somers Tracts*, 1897, pp.558-560.

13. Chope, R. Pearse, *New Light on Sir Richard Grenville*, 1917, p.213; D. B. Quinn, *The Voyage and Colonizing Enterprises of Sir Humphrey Gilbert*, 1940, pp. 156-172.

14. See Notes 1 and 4.

15. D. B. Quinn, *Raleigh and the British Empire*, 1947, p. 144.

16. J. T. Gilbert, *The Manuscripts of Charles Haliday, esq.of Dublin, Acts of the Privy Council of Ireland 1556-1571*, 1897, p. 215.

17. *The Maritime Seige of Malta*, 1965, pp. 6, 7; J. Coudy, *The Huguenot Wars*, 1969, p. 46.

18. *Hakluyt's Voyages*, 1890, Vol. III, p.165; W. C. Gosling, *Labrador*, n.d., p. 103.

19. J. A. Williamson, *Hawkins of Plymouth*, 1949, pp. 101-102.

20. J. A. Williamson, *Hawkins of Plymouth*, 1949, 201-202; G. H. Bushnell, *Sir Rich Gren*, 1936, pp. 113-116.

Endnotes 155

21. R. P. Chope, *New Light on Sir Rich Gren*, 1917, pp. 220-221; J. A. Williamson, *Hawkins of Plymouth*, 1949, pp. 201-202.

22. *Ibid.*

23. J. A. Williamson, *The Tudor Age*, 1953, p. 325.

24. Field Trip to Bideford 1975; James Christie, April 1949, Letter.

25. J. A. Williamson, *Hawkins of Plymouth*, 1949, pp. 201-202.

26. Field Trip to Buckland Abbey 1975; Alex A. Cumming, *Buckland Abbey*, p. 3.

27. Charles Kingsley, *Westward Ho.*, 1854, pp. 29-30; D. B. Quinn, ed., *Richard Hakluyt, Virginia Voyages*, 1973, p. xii.

28. D. B. Quinn, e.d., *The Roanoke Voyages 1548-1590*, 1955, p. 728, p. xxii.

29. J. E. Neale, J. E., *The Elizabethan House of Commons*, 1949, p. 301.

30. D. B. Quinn, e.d., *The Roanoke Voyages*, 1955, Vol. II, p.499.

31. G. H. Bushnell, *Sir Richard Grenville*, 1936, pp. 172-173.

32. D. B. Quinn, e.d. *The Roanoke Voyages*, 1955, Vol. II, p. 499.

33. J. A. Williamson, *The Tudor Age*, 1953, p. 325.

34. D. B Quinn, e.d. *The Roanoke Voyages*, 1955, Vol. II, p. 499.

35. J. I. Doedye, *Bideford Parish Register*, Vol. I, 1878.

36. D.B. Quinn, e.d. *The Roanoke Voyages* , 1955, Vol. II, p. xxiii.

37. W. L. Clowes, *The Royal Navy*, 1897, Vol. I, p. 495.

38. G. A. Morris, October 24, 1975, Letter.

39. G. H. Bushnell, *Sir Richard Grenville*, 1936, p. 208.

40. W. L. Clowes, *The Royal Navy*, 1897, Vol. I, p. 495.

41. D. B. Quinn, e.d., *The Roanoke Voyages 1584-1590*, 1955, p. 728.

42. I. Inkgle Doedye, *Bideford Parish Register*, 1878, p. 16.

43. V. Klagill, *Fugger News Letter*, 1926, p. 791.

44. J. K. Laughton, *State Papers Relating to the Defeat of the Spanish Armada*, 1558, Vol. I, p. 334.

45. W. L, Clowes, *The Royal Navy*, 1937, Vol.I, p. 495.

46. Christopher Ricks, ed, *Poems of Alfred Lloyd Tennyson*, "The Revenge", 1892, p. 681.

47. M. Ascott, *Bideford Parish Church*, 1950, p. 9.

48. M. Ascott, *Bideford Parish Church*, 1950, p. 9; Field trip to Bideford, 1975.

9 Bess Throckmorton Raleigh

1. *DNB*, s. v. Sir Nicholas Throckmorton, 1917.

2. H. W. Chapman, *Lady Jane Grey*, 1962, p. 155.

3. V. A. Wilson, *Queen Elizabeth's Maids of Honor and Ladies of the Privy Chamber*, 1922, p. 132.

4. *DNB*, s. v. Elizabeth, 1917.

5. *Ibid.*

6. G. B. Harrison, *The Elizabethan Journals*, 1938, pp. 1, 54.

7. Alex A. Cumming, *Buckland Abbey*, 1972.

8. Marcus Knight, *Exeter Cathedral*, 1974, pp. 3-14.

9. Field trip to Hayes Barton, 1977.

10. *Select Charters of Trading Companies 1530-1607*, p. 21; *DNB*, s. v. Sir Humphrey Gilbert.

11. *DNB*, s. v. Sir Humphrey Gilbert; *DNB* s. v. John Davys, 1917.

12. Henry R.Wagner, *Sir Francis Drake's Voyage around the World*, 1926, p 5.

13. Walter Raleigh, *The English Voyages of the Sixteenth Century*, 1906, p. 59; D. B. Quinn, *The Voyages and Colonising Enterprises of Sir Humphrey Gilbert*, 1940, pp. 488, 489.

14. D. B. Quinn, e.d., *The Voyages . . . Sir Humphrey Gilbert*, 1940, pp. 488, 489.

15. J. A. Williamson, *The Tudor Age*, 1593, p. 354.

16. Samuel Hopkins, *The Puritans and Queen Elizabeth*, 1865, Vol. I, p. 141.

17. See Note 15.

18. *DNB*, s. v. John Davis; Albert Hastings Markham, *A Life of John Davis the Navigator*, 1880, p. 24.

19. *DNB*, s. v. Raleigh, 1917.

20. See Note 3.

21. V. A. Wilson, *Queen Elizabeth's Maids*, 1922, p. 142.

Endnotes

22. *Ibid.*

23. *DNB,* s. v. Sir Walter Raleigh, 1917.

24. G. B. Harrison, *The Elizabethan Journals,* 1938, Vol. I, p. 134.

25. *DNB,* s. v. Sir Walter Raleigh, 1917.

26. G. M. Brydon, *Virginia's Mother Church,* 1947, pp. 406-407; *DNB,* s. v. Sir Walter Raleigh.

27. G. B. Harrison, *The Elizabethan Journals,* 1938, p. 150.

28. Francis L. Hawkes, *History of North Carolina,* 1859, pp. 51, 52.

29. J. D. (Attributed to Sir John Dodderidge), *The Laws .. or Women's Rights,* 1632.

30. Edward Edwards, *Lives of the Founders of the British Museum,* 1868, pp. 464-467.

31. G. B. Harrison, *The Eliz. Journals,* 1938, Vol. I, p. 172.

32. *DNB,* s. v. Sir Walter Raleigh, 1917.

33. D. B. Quinn, *Raleigh and the British Empire,* 1947, pp. 162-164.

34. *Hakluyt's Collection of Early Voyages,* 1892, Vol. III, Part 2, p. 32.

35. *DNB,* s. v. Sir Walter Raleigh, 1917.

36. V. I. Harlow, ed., *The Discoveries of Guiana, Sir Walter Raleigh,* 1928, pp. 5-84.

37. G. B. Harrison, *Elizabethan Journals,* 1938, p. 172.

38. V. T. Harlow, *Discoveries of Guiana,* 1928, pp. 5-84.

39. A. Cayley, Jr., *Life of Sir WAlter Raleigh,* 1806, Vol. II, p. 36.

40. E. Edwards, *Life of Sir Walter Raleigh,* 1868, pp. 464-467.

41. D. B. Quinn, *Raleigh and the British Empire,* 1947, pp. 219-220.

42. Edwared P. Cheyeny, *A History of England from the Defeat of the Armada to the Death of Elizabeth,* 1948, Vol.II, p. 568.

43. *Ibid.*

44. E. Edwards, *Life of Sir Walter Raleigh,* 1868, p. 312.

45. A. Cayley, *Life of Sir Walter Raleigh,* 1806, Vol. II, p. 36.

46. A. Clifford, *Diary,* 1923, p. xxiii.

47. Thomas Birch, *The Works of Sir Walter Raleigh, kt.,* 1849, Vol. I, p. 26, p. 27.

48. *DNB*, s. v. Sir Walter Raleigh, 1917.

49. V. A. Wilson, *Queen Elizabeth's Maids*, 1922, p. 142; *The Tower of London*, 1974.

50. A. Cayley, *Life of Raleigh*, 1806, p.172; T. Birch, *The Works of Raleigh*, 1849, Vol. II, p. 107.

51. J. D., "Sir Walter Raleigh, the Valiant," n. d.

10 Eleanor White Dare

1. John Derrick, "Image of Ireland," *Somers Tract*, 1809, Vol. I, pp. 558-559.

2. J. Horace Round, *Peerage and Pedigree*, (from Machyn's Diary, 1566, pp. 58-62.

3. Dorothea Townsend, *The Life and Letters of the Great Erl of Cork*, 1904, pp.317-38.

4. Hamilton McMillan, *Sir Walter Raleigh's Lost Colony*, 1888, pp. 11-24.; See Note 1.

5. Thomas L. Hartman, Letter from Department of Commerce, Manteo, N. C., June 28, 1982.

6. Samuel A. Ashe, *Biographical History of North Carolina*, 1906, p. 10.

7. *Ibid.*

8. See Note 3.

9. *DNB*, s. v. Sir Henry Sidney, 1917; John Derrick, "Image of Ireland," *Somers Tracts*, 1809, Vol. I, pp. 558-559.

10. Peter Force, *Tracts. . .relating to North America from Discovery to 1776*, 1838, Vol. III, No. 5, pp. xvii-xviii.

11. D. B. Quinn, ed., *The Roanoke Voyages 1548-1590*, 1955, Vol. I, p. 445.

12. See Note 9.

13. S. A. Ashe, *Biographical History of North Carolina*, 1906, p.10; P. Force, *Tracts*, 1838, Vol. III, No. 5; Roger Granville, *History of Bideford*, 1883, p. 28.

14. D. B. Quinn, *Raleigh's Voyages*, 1995, Vol. II, pp. 499-500.

15. Richard Hakluyt, *Principal Navigations*, 1904, p. 128, ff.

16. *Ibid.*

17. D. B. Quinn, *England and the Discovery of America 1481-1620*, 1974, p. xxii.

18. *Ibid.*

19. Theodore de Bry, *Arts in Virginia*, 1973, p.2.

20. D. B. Quinn, ed., *Roanoke Voyages*, 1955, Vol. II, p. 523.

Endnotes

21. See Note 16.

22. J. A. Williamson, *The Observations of Sir Richard Hawkins, kt.* 1933, p. 151.

23. D. B. Quinn, ed., *Roanoke Voyages*, 1955, Vol. II, pp. 499-500.

24. D. B. Quinn, ed., *Roanoke Voyages*, 1955, Vol. I, frontpiece.

25. H. McMillan, *Raleigh's Lost Colony*, 1888, p. 24.

26. John Clark Ridpath, *A Popular History of Virginia*, 1889, p. 83

27. See Note 20.

28. H. McMillan, *Ral. Lost Colony*, 1888, pp. 18, 27.

29. D. B. Quinn, ed. *England and the Discovery of America*, 1973, p. xxiii.

30. See Note 28.

31. D. B. Quinn, ed., *England and the Discovery of America*, 1973, p. xxiii; S. A. Ashe, *Biographical History of North Carolina*, 1906, Vol. IV, p.42.

32. See Note 29.

33. D. B. Quinn, *England and the Discovery of America.*, 1973, pp. 115-116.

34. Theodore de Bry, *Arts in Virginia.*, 1973, p.2, pp. 30-32.

35. See Note 35.

36. *DNB*, s. v. John White, 1917.

37. D. B. Quinn, *England and the Discovery of America*, 1973, p. xxv.

38. L. B. Wright and M. Tingling, ed., *William Byrd of Virginia*, 1958, p. 553.

39. G. H. Bushnell, *Sir Richard Grenville*, 1936, pp. 243, 244, 246.

40. K. R. Andrews, *Elizabethan Privateering*, 1964, p. 195.

41. *Customs Records of the Court of Barnstaple, 1599.*

42. C. M. Lewis and A. J. Loomie, *The Spanish Jesuit Mission in Virginia 1540-1572*, 1953, p. 262.

43. *DNB*, s. v. John White, 1917.

44. Joseph Brittingham, *The First Trading Post in Virginia 1540-1572*, 1947, p. 10.

45. John Fiske, *Virginia and Her Neighbors*, 1897, Vol. I, p. 101.

46. J.D. (John Dodderidge), *Laws...Women's Rights*, 1632.

47. S. A. Ashe, Biographical History of North Carolina, 1906, p. 15.

48. Edward Arber, ed., *Travels and Works of John Smith*, 1910, p. 55.

49. *Ibid.*

50. H. McMillan, *Raleigh's Lost Colony*, 1888, pp. 18-27; S. A. Ashe, *Biographical History of North Carolina*, 1906, p. 15.

51. Psalm 23, *The Holy Bible*, Oxford Press, England, n.d.

MANUSCRIPTS, CALENDARS, LISTS, AND RECORDS

Advowson from King James I to John Darracott and Nicholas Downe, Devon Record Office, 1607.

Arber, Edward. *Illustrative Documents of the London Company of Virginia.* London: Edward Arber, n. d.

_____, editor. *Travels and Works of John Smith.* Edinburg, J. Grant, 1910.

Archaelogia Americana: Transactions and Collections of American Antiquarian Society, "Newport's Discoveries in Virginia," Vol. IV. Published for the Society, 1860.

Barnstaple Parish Register 1528-1812. Thomas Wainwright, editor. Exeter: James G. Commin, 1903.

Bibliotheque Landsdown. Edited, Sir Henry Ellis and Frances Douce, Part I. London: Director of Records Commission, n.d.

Bideford Parish Register, I. Ingle Doedye, 1878.

Birch, Thomas. *The Works of Sir Walter Raleigh, kt.* Vol. I. London: Tully's Hesf, 1751.

The Camden Miscellany. *Officers of the Royal Historical Society.* London, 1902.

Camden Society, *The Knights Hospitallers,* n.d.

Chalmers, *The Works of English Poets.* London: J. Johnson, 1810.

Christie, James, Letter to Mrs. F. M. Timmins. April 6, 1949.

Clifford, Lady Anne. *The Diary of the Lady Anne Clifford, with an introductory Note by V. Sackville-West.* London: William Heinemann, Ltd., 1923.

Colonial Records of Virginia: Elizabeth City, 1622, edited by R. F. Walker, 1894.

Cotton Manuscript. 52786. British Museum. n. d.

Customs Records of the Court of Barnstaple. Public Record Office. London, 1599.

de Courcy,. Pol. Potier. *Dictionaire Heraldique de Bretagne, Complement de tous les Noilaires de Amoraux aux de cette Province.* Edward De Bergevin. Rennes: J. Philton and L.Herve, 1895.

de Bry, Theodore. *Arts in Virginia*, Richmond: Virginia Museum, Spring, 1973

Derrick, John. "Image of Ireland," *Somers Tracts*. Coll. Walter Scott Esq., 2nd. ed. London: t. Cadell and W. Davies, 1809.

Diary of Dr. Dee. n.p., n.d.

Dictionaire de la Noblesse dan de Crocefe de lecar en Bearn 1738.

Dictionary of National Biography, edited by Leslie Stephen and Sidney Lee. London: Oxford University, 1917.

J. D. (Attributed by Thomas Wentworth to Sir John Dodderidge.) *The Lawes, Resolutions, or the Lawes Provision for Women, or Women's Rights*. London: n. p., 1632.

_____. (Sir John Dodderidge) *Tracts, 1680.*

_____. *A Law of Advowsons and Church Living*. London, p. h.

_____. "The Works of Raleigh the Valiant." n. d., Library of Congress.

Edwards, Edward. *Lives of the Founders of the British Museum*. London: Tucker, Patycote Row, 1870.

_____. *The Life of Sir Walter Raleigh based on Contemporary Documents preserved in the Rolls House, the Privy Council Office, hatfield House*, 2 vols. Macmillan and Co., 1868.

Exeter Historical Manuscripts Commission. *Report on the Records of the City of Exeter*. London, 1916.

Force, Peter. *Tracts and Other Papers Relating Principally to the Origin, Settlement and Progress of the Colonies in North America, from the Discovery of the Country to the Year 1776*. Vol. II and III. Washington: Peter Force, 1838.

Gilbert, J. T., ed. *The Manuscripts of Charles Haliday, Esq. of Dublin, Acts of the Privy Council of Ireland, 1556-1571*. London: Eire and Spottisworde, 1897.

Hakluyt Society Extra Series. No. XXXIX. n.d.

Hakluyt's Voyages, Hakluyt's Collection of the EarlyVoyages,Travels, and Discoveries of the English Nation. Vol. 3. London: R. H. Evans, 1890.

Hakluyt, Richard. *The Principal Navigations, Traffiques and Discoveries of the English Nation*, Vols. III, VI. Glasgow: James McLehose and Sons, 1904.

Harlow, V. T., editor. *The Discoverie of Guiana, Sir Walter Raleigh*, ed. N. M. Penze. London: The Argonaut Press, 1928.

Harrison, G. B. *The Elizabethan Journals*. London: George Routledge and Sons, 1938.

Hartman, Thomas L. Letter, Manteo, North Carolina: Department of Interior, 1982.

High Court of Admiralty 13/30, 24/59, 25/3. Public Record Office. London, n.d.

Manuscripts, Calendars, Lists and Letters 163

Historical Manuscripts Commission. *Middleton MSS: Report of Manuscripts of Lord Middleton preserved at Wollaton Hall,Northamptonshire.* His Majestiy's Stationery Office, 1911.

_____. *Report on the Manuscripts of Lord de L'isle and Dudley Preserved at Penshurst Place.* Vol. I, 1925. London.

_____. *Duke of Rutland* (Nobility Claim), Vol. IV, 1905.

The Holy Bible, Old and New Testaments. Onward Press, Richmond, Va., n.d.

The Hymnbook. Presbyterian Church in United States. Richmond: MCMLV

Index of Wills and Administrations proved in the Archdeaconery of Barnstaple. Courtesy of N.S.E. Pugsley, Exeter City Library.

Inderwick, Frederick Andrew, editor. *The Inner Temple, Its Early History as Illustrated by its Records 1505-1603.* London: Stevens and Sons, 1896.

Ingpen, Arthur Robert, K. C. *Middle Temple Bench Book.* London: n. p., 1912.

Izacke, Richard. *Remarkable Antiquities of the City of Exeter.* 1724.

Karwill, Victor. *The Fugger News Letters 1568-1605.* London: John Lane, 1926.

Lang, Andrew. *Mystery of Mary Stewart.* New York and Bombay: Longman,Green and Co, 1902.

Laughton, John Knox. *State Papers relating to the Defeat of the Spanish Armada.* Navy Record Society, 1894.

Leeds Castle, Illustrated History and Guide to the Rooms. Maidstone, Kent: Leeds Castle Foundation, 1985.

Lists and Analysis Foreign State Papers, Elizabeth I. Vol II, July 1590-May 1591. London: His Majesty's Stationery Office, 1969.

Manhart, Roland. *English Commerce and Exploration in the Reign of Elizabeth.* Philadelphia: University of Pennsylvania. 1927.

Markham, Clements R. *The Journal of Christopher Columbus and Documents relating to the Voyages of John Cabot and Gaspar Corte Real.* London: Hakluyt Society, 1893.

_____. *The Life of John Davis the Navigator.* London: Hakluyt Society, 1880.

Nuttall, Zelia. *New Light on Drake, A Collection of Documents relating to his voyage of Circumnavigation 1577-1580.* London: Hakluyt, 1904.

Official Guide to Windsor Castle. 1974.

Oswyn Murray Collection. Wills 3/36. Exeter Public Library, Devon.

Pacta Hibernia, or a History of the Wars in Ireland during the reign of Queen Elizabeth, especially within the province of Munster under the Government of Sir George Carew. Standish O'Grady, ed. London; Downey and Co., 1896.

Pigafetta. *The First voyage Round the World by Magellan. . .With Notes and an Introduction*, Lord Stanley of Aderley. London: Hakluyt Society, 1874.

Plymouth Municipal Records. R. N. Worth. Plymouth: Willia and Sons. Plymouth, Devon, 1813.

Public Record Office. CO/1/46, CO/42. Great Britain. n. d.

Purchase, Samuel. *Hakluiyt Posthumus.* N.Y.: James McLehese and Son, 1600.

Quinn, David Beers, editor. *Richard Hakluyt, Virginia Voyages from Hakluyt.* London: Oxford University Press, 1973.

_____, editor. *The Roanoke Voyages 1548-1590.* 2 vols. London: Hakluyt Society, 1955.

_____, editor. *The Voyages and Colonising Enterprises of Sir Humphrey Gilbert.* 2 vols. London: Hakluyt Society, 1940.

Reprint of Barnstaple Records. J. R. Chanter and Thomas Wainwright, Vol. II, Barnstaple: A. L. Barnes, 1900.

Ribaut, Jena. *The Whole and True Discoureye of Terra Florida, A Facsimilie Reprint of the London Edition of 1563; Notes by Bibliography by Jeanette Thurber Conner.* Florida State Historical Society, 1927.

Ricks, Christopher, editor. *Poems of Alfred L. Tennyson,* "The Revenge." London: Longmans 1892.

Scott, A. F., *The Tudor Age.* London: Whiteline Publisher, 1975.

Scott, Walter, Esq. *Somers Tracts, a Collection of Scarce and Valuable tracts on the most interesting and entertaining subjects.* 2nd edition. Vol. I. London: T. Cadell and W. Davies, 1809.

_____. *Kenilworth, Leicester's Commonwealth.* N. Y. : F. A. Crowell, n.d.

Scottish Confession of Faith.

Select Charters of Trading Companies 1530-1607. Selden Society.

Townshend, Dorothea. *The Life and Letters of the Great Earl of Cork.* London: Duckworth and Co., 1904.

Westminster Shorter Catechism. General Assembly of Presbyterian Church in the U. S. December 4, 1861, Presbyterian Committee of Publication. Richmond, Virginia, 1861.

Woodruff, C. Evelyn, editor. *Kent Records. Calendar of Institutions by the Chapter of Cnteryur Sede Vacante.* Kent Archaelogical Society. 1923.

Worth, R. N. *Calendar of Plymouth Municipal Records. 1893.*

Wright, Irene A., editor. *Documents concerning English voyages to the Spanish Main 1569-1580.* London, 1932.

_____. *Further English Voyages to Spanish America 1583-1594.* London: Hakluyt Society, 1951.

_____. *Spanish Documents Concerning English Voyages to the Caribbean, 1527-1568.* 2nd series. Hakluyt Society, 1929.

Wright, Louis B. and Marion Tingling, editors. *William Byrd of Virginia.* N. Y.: Oxford University Press, 1958.

Wyatt, Capt. *The Voyage of Robert Dudley, to the West Indies 1594-95.* London: George F. Warner, 1899.

BIBLIOGRAPHY

Abbot, John S. C. *Makers of History*, Akron Ohio: Superior Printing Co., 1942.

Addleshaw, Percy, *The Cathedral Church of Exeter*. London: George Bell and Sons, 1899.

_____ . *Sir Philip Sidney*. New York: G. P. Putnam's Sons, 1909.

Albin, J. *History of the Isle of Wight*, Newport: 1975

Andrews, Kenneth R. *Elizabethan Privateering during the Spanish War 1585-1603*. Cambridge; University Press, 1964

_____ . *English Privateering Voyages to the West Indies, 1588-1595*. Cambridge, University Press. 1959, 1964.

Arber, Edward. *An English Garner*. Westminster: Archibald Constable and Co., n.d.

_____ . *Illustrative Documents of the London Virginia Company*. London: Edward Arber, n.d.

_____ , editor. *John Smith, 1588-1631*. Birmingham: 1884.

Ascott, Major. *An Easy Guide to Bideford Parish Church*, n. p. 1950.

Ashe, Samuel A. *Biographical History of North Carolina*. Vol. IV, Greensoro, N. C.: Van Nopper, 1906.

Baird, Charles W. *History of Huguenot Emigration to America*. Baltimore Regional Publishing Co., 1966.

Baird, Henry M. *History of the Huguenots in France, 1875-93*. New York: Charles Scribners, 1879.

Barbour, Philip L. *The Jamestown Voyages under the First Charter 1606-1609*. Cambridge: Hakluyt Sons, 1969.

_____ . *The Complete Works of Captain John Smith, 1580-1611*. n. d.

Bancroft, George. *History of the United States from the Discovery of the American Continent*. Vol. I. Boston: Charles C. Little and James Brown, 1845.

Beltz, George Frederick. *Memorial of the Most Noble Order of the Garter*. London, Pickering, 1841.

Bennett, John. *Seventeenth Century Isle of Wight County, Virginia*.

Chateaux of the Loire, ed. Micheline Tyre Co., Ltd., 1974.

Chettle, G. H. *Hampton Court Palace.* London: Her Majesty's Stationery Office, 1975.

Cheyney, Edward P. *A History of England from the Defeat of the Armada to the Death of Elizabeth.* Vol. I and II. New York: Peter Smith, 1948.

Chope, R. Pearce. *New Light on Sir Richard Grenville.* 1917.

Clowes, William Laird. *The Royal Navy.* Vol. I. London: Sampson Low, Marston and Co., 1897.

Corbett, Julian S. *Drake and the Tudor Navy.* Vol. I and II. London: Longmans, Green., 1889.

_____. *The Successors of Drake.* London: Longmans, Green and Co., 1900.

Cotter, John L. *Archological Excavations at Jamestown.* Washington: U. S. dept. of Interior, 1958.

Cotton, William. *An Elizabethan Guild of the City of Exeter.* Exeter: William Pollard, 1873.

Coudy, Julian, ed., *The Huguenot Wars.* Philadelphia: Chilton Book Co., 1969.

Crofts, Pauline. *The Spanish Company.* London Record Society. Chatham, Great Britain: W. L.& J. Mackay, Ltd., 1973.

Cumming, Alex A. *Buckland Abbey.* Norwich, Great Britain: Jarold and Son, Ltd., 1972.

Donaldson, Gordon. *The First Trial of Mary Queen of Scots.* Stein and Day, 1969.

Drake, Samuel Adam. *The making of New England.* N. Y., Scribners, 1888.

Dumas, Alexander. *Three Musketeers.* Bungay, Soffolk: Richard Clay and Sons, 1906.

Edinburg Review, "A Brief discovery of the troubles at Frankfort in the year 1554. . ." Vol. LXXV. Edinburg: Ballantyne and Hughes.

Fiske, John. *Old Virginia and Her Neighbors.* Boston: Houghton, Mifflin and Co., 1897.

Fleming, David Hay. *Mary, Queen of Scots.* London: Hodder and Stoughton. MDCCXCVIII.

Fraser, Antonia. *Mary Queen of Scots.* N. Y.: Delacourt Press, 1969.

"French Protestantism." *John Hopkins Stuidies.* Vol. 36, 1918.

Froude, James Anthony. *The English in the West Indies.* New York: Charles Scribners Sons, 1900.

_____. *English Seamen in the Sixteenth Century, Lectures delivered at Oxford Easter Terms, 1893-4.* Charles Scribners Sons. 1895.

Gardiner, Samuel R. *A Student's History of England.* New York: Longmans, Green, 1904.

Garrett, Christina Hollowell. *The Marian Exiles.* Cambridge: University Press, 1938.

Gasgoine, Christian. *Castles of Britain.* New York: Thomes and Harlein, 1980.

Goaman, Muriel. *Old Bideford and District.* Bristol, England: E. M. and A. G. Cox, 1968.

Bibliography

Goldsmid, Edmund Munden. *The Last Fight of the Revenge.* Edinburgh: Private Press, 1866.

Gookin, Warner F.D. "Who was Bartholomew Gosnold?" *W & M Quarterly*, 3rd series, 1949.

Gosling, W. C. *Labrador.* Toronto: The Musson Book Co., n.d.

Granville, Rev. Roger. *The History of Bideford.* Bideford: W. Crosbie Coles, 1883.

Hawkes, Francis L., DD. *History of North Carolina.* Vol. I and II. Fayetteville, N.C.: E. J. Hale and Son, 1859.

Henry, Paul. *Life and Times of John Calvin.* N.Y.: Robert Carter and Sons, 1853.

Hopkins, Samuel. *The Puritans and Queen Elizabeth.* N.Y.: Anson D. F. Randolph & Co., (1865).

Hume, Martin A. S. *The Year After the Armada.* London. 1896.

Ireland, W. H. *Memories of Henry the Great.* Harding, Triphook & Leparel, 1824.

Jenkins, J. T. *A History of Whalers, Fishermen.* Witherby, W. C., 1921.

Kelly, Cabel Guyier. *French Protestantism, 1599-1652,* Vol. 36.

King, Edward and Luke, Harry. *Knights of St. John.* St. John's Gate, E. C. I., 1967.

Kingsley, Charles. *Westward Ho, or the Adventures of Amias Leigh.* London: McMillan and Co., 1911.

Kohl, J. G. *Collections of Maine Historical Society.* 2nd Series, Vol. I. Portland: Bailey and Noyes, 1869.

Knight, The Very Rev. Marcus. *Exeter Cathedral.* London: Pitkin Pictorials, 1974.

Laval, Stephen Able. *History of Reference in France.* London: 1737.

Lewis, Clifford M. and Loomie, Albert J. *The Spanish Jesuit Mission in Virginia 1540-1572.* The Virginia Historical Society. Chapel Hill, N.C.: The University of North Carolina Press, 1953.

Linkletter, Eric. *The Royal House.* N. Y.: Doubleday, 1970.

Lord Brook *Life of Sir Philip Sidney.* Kent: Private Press of Lee Priory, Johnson and Warren, 1816.

Lord Russell of Liverpool. *Henry of Navarre and the Huguenots.* N. Y.: Prayer, 1961.

MacCaffrey, Wallace T. *Exeter 1540-1640, The Growth of an English Country Town.* Cambridge: Harvard University Press, 1958.

McMillan, Hamilton. *Sir Walter Raleigh's Lost Colony.* Wilson, N.C.: 1888.

Manhart, Roland. *English Commerce and Exploration in the Reign of Elizabeth.* Philadelphia: University of Pennsylvania. 1927.

The Maritime Siege of Malta 1565. National Maritime Museum. London: McCorquodale Printers Ltd. n.d.

Markham, Albert Hastings. *A Life of John Davis the Navigator.* London: Hakluyt Society. 1880.

Martin, Charles. *Les Protestants Anglais Réfugies à Geneva au temps de Calvin.* Geneva: A. Julien, 1915.

Mathew, David. *Lady Jane Grey.* Eyre Metheun. 1972.

Mattingly, Garrett. *The Armada.* Boston: Houghton Milllin Co., 1959.

Mignet, Porter. *A History of Mary Queen of Scots.* Richard Bentley, 1863.

Morley, John. *English Man of Letters, Sidney.* London: Macmillan and Co., 1906.

Morris, G. M. Letter October 24, 1975. North Devon Athenaeum, Barnstaple.

Neale, J. E. *The Elizabethan House of Commons.* London: Jonathan Cape, 1949.

Nicholas, Harris. *The Literary Remains of Lady Jane Grey.* London: Harding, Triphook and Lepora, 1825.

Nicholas, John Gough. *The Chronicle of Queen Jane and two years of Queen Mary.* Camden: 1750.

Nicholas, Sir Nicholas Harris. *The Historic Peerage of England.* London: William Courthope, 1857.

Nolan, John E. H. "Life in the Land of Basques." *National Geographic Magazine,* Feb. 1964.

Oldys, William. *The Life of Sir Walter Raleigh.* London: William Oldys, 1740.

Ormond, P. S. *Basques and their Country.* London: Simpkins, Marshall, Hamilton, Kent & Co, Ltd. 1926.

Palm, Franklin Charles. *Calvinism and the Religious Wars.* Henry Holt and Co., 1932.

Parks, George Bruner. "Richard Hakluyt and the English Voyages." *William and Mary Quarterly,* 3rd series, Vol. VI, 1949.

Pinkerton, John. *Voyages and Travels.* London: Longman, Hurst, Reese, & Orme. 1808.

Prescott, William H. *History of the Conquest of Peru.* 2 vol. New York: Harper and Bros. 1882.

Purchas His Pilgrims, extra series. Vol. XVIII. Glasgow: Hakluyt Society, 1905.

Quinn, David B(eers). *England and the Discovery of America, 1481-1620.* New York: Alfred A. Knopf, 1974.

_____. *Raleigh and the British Empire.* London: Hodder and Stoughton, Ltd. 1947.

Raleigh, Walter. *The English Voyages of the Sixteenth Century.* Glasgow: James MacLehose and Sons, 1906.

Bibliography

Read, Conyers. *Mr. Secretary Walsingham and the Policy of Queen Elizabeth.*3 vols. Cambridge: Harvard University Press, 1925.

Ridpath, John Clark. *A Popular History of the United States of America.* New York: Hunt and Eaton, 1889.

Risdon, Tristram. *The Chronology and Description of the Courts of Devon.* London: E. Curll, 1714.

Ritter, Robert. *Le Pay de Bearn.* Pau: J. Delman et Cu., 1924.

Round, J. Horace. *Peerage and Pedigree.* (from Machyn's Diary), 1566.

Rowse, A. L. *The England of Elizabeth.* New York: Mamillan and Co., 1941.

_____. *Sir Richard Grenville of the Revenge.* New York: Houghton-Mifflin, 1937.

Sams, Conway Whittle, B.L. *The Conquest of Virginia.* Norfolk: Keyser Doherty, 1924.

Saunders, William L. "Colonial Records of North Carolina," *Virginia Magazine of History and Biography.* Vol. VII, 1713-1728. Raleigh: P. M. Hold, 1886.

Shelton, R. A. "Raleigh as a Geographer," *Virginia Magazine of History,* Vol. 71.

Shirley, John W. "Sir Walter Raleigh's Guiana Finances," *Huntington Library Quarterly,* Vol. 3., 1989-90.

Simon, Andrew L. *The Noble Grapes and Great Wines of France.* Toronto: Canada, McGraw Hill, 1947.

Selincourt, Hugh de. *Life of Raleigh.* New York: G. P. Putnam's Sons. 1908.

Taylor, E. G. R. "More Light on Drake: 1577-80." *Mariner's Mirror.* April, 1930.

_____. "The Missing Draft Project of Drake's voyage of 1577-8." *Geographical Journal.* Vol. LXXV, No. 1, January, 1930.

_____. *Tudor Geography 1485-1583.* London: Methuen and Co. Ltd., 1930.

Tennyson, Alfred Lloyd. *Poems of Alfred Lloyd Tennyson, "The Revenge."* Edited, Christopher Ricks. (London): Longman, 1972.

Terrance, Charles. *Fountainebleau Palace.* National Museum: Paris, 1944.

The Tower of London. Department of the Environment. London: Her Majesty's Stationery Office, 1974.

Travis, Robert Jesse. *The Travis (Travers) Family and its Allies, etc.* Savannah, Georgia: The Author, 1954.

Vertot, Rene Aubert de, abbe. *The History of the Knights Hospitallers of St. John of Jerusalem.* Edinburgh: A. Donaldson, 1770.

Wagner, Henry R. *Sir Francis Drake's Voyage Around the World.* Glendale, Cal.: The Arthur H. Clark Co., 1926.

Watkins, C. Malcolm. *North Devon Pottery and its Export to America in the 17th Century.* Washington, D. C.: Smithsonian, 1960.

Weeks, Stephen B. *The Lost Colony of Roanoke.* New York: Knickerbocker Press, 1891.

Wheeler, Elizabeth Darracott. *Sir John Dodderidge, Celebrated Barrister of Britain 1555-1628.* Mellen Research University Press, 1992.

Wheeler, John Hill. *Historical Sketches of North Carolina.* Baltimore, 1946.

Willert, P. F. *Henry of Navarre and the Huguenots.* New York: G. P. Putnam's Sons, 1893.

Williamson, Dr. G. C. *George, Third Earl of Cumberland 1553-1685.* Cambridge, University Press, 1920.

Williamson, James A. *Hawkins of Plymouth.* London: Adam and Charles Black, 1949.

_____. *The Obwervations of Sir Richard Hawkins, Kt.: The Hawkins Voyages.* London: The Argonaut Press, 1933.

_____. *The Tudor Age.* London: Longman, Green and Co., 1953.

Wilson, Violet A. *Queen Elizabeth's Maids of Honor and Ladies of the Privy Chamber.* New York: E.P. Dutton and Co., 1922.

Worth, R.N. F.G.S. *A History of Devonshire.* London: Elliot Stock, 1885.

Wroth, Lawrence C. *The Voyages of Giovanni da Verrazzano 1524-1528.* New Haven: Yale University Press, 1970.

Index

A
Allington Castle, 14
Amazon, 20, 59, 74, 119, 120
Antoine de Bourbon, 25, 27, 29, 30
Archard, Joyce, 126
Argyll, Earl of, 42, 43, 44, 46, 47, 51, 52
Arrundell, Alexander, 103
Arrundell, John, 106
Asham, Robert, 4
Aylmer, Mr., 2

B
Babington, 54
Barnstaple, 72, 84, 85, 98, 106, 108, 128, 129, 139
Bassett, Arthur, 103
Bayley, Roger, 128
Bertie, Richard, 19
Bideford, 84, 97, 98, 100, 101, 103, 105, 106, 107, 109, 110, 128, 133, 134, 136, 139
Bodleigh, John, 18, 20
Boleyn, Queen Anne, 5, 8, 13, 14, 16
Boleyn, Thomas, 13, 14
Bothwell, Earl of, see Hepburn, James
Bradgate Castle, 2
Brandon, Catherine, 1, 9
Brandon, Charles, 1, 60
Brandon, Frances, Dutchess of Suffolk, 1, 2 6
Brass Mount, 9
Bucher, Martin, 3
Buckland Abbey, 84, 104, 105

C
Cabot, John, 98, 102
Cabot, Sebastian, 59, 131
Calvin, John, 3, 4, 11, 16, 17, 25, 28, 38
Calvinists, 3, 18, 20, 24, 34, 36, 37, 75
Cape Hatteras, 125, 131, 134, 136, 137
Canongate Palace, 46
Cardinal of Bourbon, 43
Carlisle, Christopher, 101
Carey, George, governor, 136
Casket papers, 55
Cathay Company, 59, 101, 102, 104
Catherine of Aragon, Queen of England, 9, 13, 15, 22, 60
Catherine d' Medici, 27, 36
Catholic, 2, 13, 15, 17, 20, 25, 28, 31, 32, 33, 35, 37, 39, 40, 41, 42, 43, 44, 46, 47, 52
Cavendish, Thomas, 107
Cecil, Sir William, Lord Burghly, 5, 7, 23, 45, 53, 54, 59, 72, 77, 78, 92; wife, 92

Chapman, Alis, 126
Charles IX, 43
Charles Fort, 73
Chateau Coarraze, 26
Chenonceau Castle, 71
Chesapeake Bay, 68, 110, 128, 130, 133, 135, 136, 137
Church of England, 113, 128
Clifford, Lady Anne, Diary, 83, 86
Clifford, George, Earl of Cumberland, 62, 83, 85, 86; wife, see Margaret Clifford
Clifford, Henry, 86
Clifford, Francis, 93
Clifford, Margaret, Countess of Cumberland, 83-95, 138
Clovelly, 94
Coligny, Gaspard, admiral, 16, 18, 29, 61, 73, 75, 79, 80, 99
Columbus, 70, 130
Compton Castle, 113
Cooke, captain, 133
Cooper, Christopher, 128
Cork, 100
Cortez, Governor of Mexico, 114
Courtenay, Edward, 73, 84, 106
Covedale, Miles, 4, 84
Cowgate Palace, 41
Cox, Dr. Richard, 5
Cramner, Thomas, archbishop, 15
Cranborne, 58
Croatan,"CRO," 130, 132, 135

D
Dacre, Anne, 86
Dare, Ananias, 125, 127, 128, 129, 133, 137
Dare, Eleanor, First Lady of Virginia, 106, 121-138
Dare, Virginia, 133, 135, 137, 138
Dare, Martin, 103
Darnley, Lord, see Stewart, Henry
Darracott House, 106
Darracott, John, Jr., admiral, 107
Darracott, William, 106, 132
D'Arricau-Bordes Castle, 26, 27, 35
Darricau, Robetus, 72
Davis, John, 62, 87, 115
Dee, John, 32, 57, 62, 83, 90, 114
de Bry, Theodore, 75
Devonshire, 58, 58, 66, 71, 72, 74, 79, 98, 99, 101, 107, 110, 113, 115, 116

Diane de Poitiers, 40
Diggs, Thomas, 103
Dodderidge, John, King's Bench, 62, 117, 123, 136
Don Antonio, 86, 88, 89, 129
Don Carlos, Emperor of Austria, 41
Don John, 41
Drake, Sir Francis, 105, 112
Duarte Castle, 41
Dudley, Guildford, 1, 5, 6, 7, 8, 9, 10, 11, 57, 59, 60
Dudley, John, Duke of Northumberland, admiral, Vicount L'Isle, 4, 5, 55, 59, 98; wife, Anne, 4, 5, 51, 52, 57
Dudley, Robert, Earl of Leicester, 41, 43, 59, 62, 74, 80; wife, see Amy Robsart
Duke of Ferrar, 43
Duke of Guise, 43
Duke of Norfolk, 43
Dumbarton Castle, 46
Dunbar Castle, 46
Durham Palace, 6

E

East Indian (Indies) Company, 83, 91, 94
Edgecombe, Pierce, 15
Edinburgh Castle, 41, 46, 50
Edward VI, 3, 4, 5, 6, 8, 15, 58, 59, 111
Eleanor of Acquitaine, 85
Elizabeth I, Queen of England, 3, 5, 13, 14, 15, 16, 18, 22, 23, 30, 40, 42, 43, 44, 47, 50, 51, 52, 53, 54, 55, 61, 62, 64, 65, 66, 67, 68, 72, 73, 74, 77, 78, 80, 81, 83, 84, 85, 86, 88, 89, 91, 92, 99, 101, 103, 106, 108, 111, 112, 114, 116, 117, 120, 121, 125, 127, 128, 130, 133
Exeter, 84, 85, 86 87, 88, 112, 115, 121, 139

F

Farrell, William, 16, 25
Fernandez, Simon, 128, 129
Fleming, Mary, 44, 46, 52
Fort Augustine, 130
Fort Caroline, 32
Fort Charles, 32
Fort Raleigh, 27, 133
Fountainbleau Palace, 25
Fullwood, William, 121
Francis I, King of France, 25, 27, 29
Francis II, King of France, 39, 40, 44
Frobisher, Martin, 23

G

Geneva, 17, 21, 22, 30, 40, 80

Gilbert, Catherine Champernown, 113
Gilbert, Adrian, 113, 114, 115
Gilbert, Bartholomew, 133
Gilbert, Lord John, 113
Gilbert, Sir Humphrey, 67, 100, 101 114, 115
Glane, Elizabeth, 126
Glasgow Castle, 44, 45, 47, 52
Gosnold, Bartholomew, 23
Greenwich Palace 7, 8, 111
Grenville, John, 119
Grenville, Mary St. Leger, 97-110, 138; children, 98
Grenville, Rebecca, 98, 107
Grenville, Sir Richard, captain-general, parliament, 23, 97, 98, 110, 114, 115, 118
Grey, Lady Jane, Queen of England, 1-11, 59, 73, 138; 111; see husband, Guildford Dudley
Grey, Sir Henry, Marquis of Dorset 1, 3, 6, 9, 59, 60; wife, Frances Brandon, see above
Grey, Katherine, 3, 5
Guernsey, 70, 74, 78, 80, 85
Guild Hall, London, 9
Guild Hall, Exeter, 84

H

Hakluyt, Rev. Richard, 23, 66
Hamiltons, 45
Hampton Court Castle, 15, 52
Hariot, Thomas, 107
Harvey, Dyonaise, 128
Hastings, Lord, 5
Hatteras, (Cape Hataroask), 125, 131, 136, 137
Hawkins, Sir John, 23
Henry II, duke of Anjou, king, 23, 30, 41, 73, 85, 116
Henry III, duke of Orleans, 43
Henry IV, King of France, 25, 27, 28, 30, 37, 67; wife, see Margaret of Valois, 35
Henry VII, 1, 43
Henry VIII, 1, 3, 4, 5; wives see Catherine of Aragon, Anne Boleyn, Jane Seymour, Katherine Parr
Henry d'Albret, King of Navarre, 25
Hepburn, James, Earl of Bothwell, 44, 45, 46, 47, 48, 49, 50 51, 52
Hepburn, Patrick, 52
Herbert, Lord, 5
Hermitage Castle, 47
Hertford, Earl of, 112
Hever Castle, Kent, 14
Hilliard, Nicholas, 20
Hispaniola Island, 130, 136
Holywood Palace, 40, 44

Index

Hooper, Dr., bishop, 4
Horsey, Sir Edward, governor, 32, 59, 80; wife, see Mademoiselle Horsey
Horsey, Francis, 72
Horsey, Jerome, 78
Horsey, Mademoiselle, 69-81, 126, 138
House of Bourbon, 26
Howard, Lord Thomas, admiral, 109, 121
Howe, George, 128
Huguenots, 22, 30, 31, 32, 33, 34, 35, 40, 70, 71, 72, 74, 75, 76, 77, 78, 79, 80, 101, 103
Huntly, 42, 45, 46, 47, 51

I

Indians, 23, 120, 125, 133, 134, 135, 136
Inuit Indian, 87
Irish chieftain, Mayor of Cork, 100
Irish, William, 126
Isabel de Rivers, 74
Isle of Wight, 74, 77, 81, 136
Issary, Bass-Navarre, 33

J

Jamaica, 85
James V, of Scotland, 39
James I of England, 3, 121, 137, 139 wife, see Anne
James de Fox, bishop, 28
Jean d' Albret, Baron de Moissen, 28; wife, Susanne de Bourbon-Busset
Jeanne d'Albret, Queen of Navarre and Bearn, 25-37, 3, 58, 64, 61, 138; wife of, see Antoinne de Bourbon
Jersey, 74, 116
Jones, Jane, 126

K

Kecoughtan, 137
Kenilworth castle, 61, 62
Kerrycurrihy estate, 99, 127
King Arthur of the Round Table, 105
King of Denmark, 43
King of Navarre, 43
King of Sweden, 43
Kirk o'Field, 42, 44, 46, 48
Knights of St. John, 15, 36, 58, 62, 97, 105, 125, 126, 130
Knights of the Garter, 62, 64, 89
Knights of Malta, 30, 58, 67, 126
Knole Castle, 93
Knollys (Knolles), Sir Francis, 32, 53, 101
Knolly, Henry, 23
Knollys, Kate, 18, 19
Knox, John, 40, 41, 46; wife Margery

L

Labrador, 101, 114
La Rochelle, 33, 34
Lane, Ralph, 106, 115
Lawrence, 108
Leeds Castle, 14
Lennox, Earl of, Dukedom of RichMond, 37, 45, 47, 48, 49, 51, 52, 53, 54; wife, Lady Lennox
Lescar, 26
Lethington, 50, 51, 54
Linlithgow Palace, 39
Lisieux Cathedral, 70
Lismore Castle, 126
Louis de Bourbon, Prince de Condé, 34
Lourdes, 28
Ludlow Castle, 65

M

Maltese Cross, 97, 98, 134
Manteo, 132, 133
Marjorie, 131
Marguerite d' Valvois, Queen of Navarre, 25, 35
Martin, John, 101
Mary of Guise, Queen Regent of Scotland, 1, 25, 44, 48, 61
Mary Queen of Scots, 39-55, 108, 136; see Francis II; Lord Darnley
Mary Tudor, Queen of England, 1, 5, 8
Melville, Robert, 51
Mermouth, Emma, 126
minister, Roanoke Island, 133
Mont Saint Michel, 70
Montevideo, 30, 81, 102
More, Sir Thomas, 66
Morton, 64
Murray, Earl of, 46

N

Navarre and Bearn, 25, 30, 31, 32, 36
Newfoundland, 29, 84, 119
New Learning, 15, 25, 26, 72
Newport, Christopher, 137
Newport Church, 81
Nicholls, John, 128
Normandy, 69, 70, 80, 81
Northam, coastal road, 98
Notre Dame Cathedral, 30, 86
Norris, L(ord), 86
Nottoway Indians, 135

O

Old Learning, 2, 70

Orinoco River, 119
Oxenham, 105
Oxford University, 62

P

Pamunkey River, 136
Panama, 85
Papacy, 15
Parr, Katherine,Queen Dowager, 3, 4, 15
Pau Castle 25, 26, 27, 28, 31
Payne, Rose, 126
Peckham, Sir George, 101
Pedro Menendez de Abila, 75
Penshurst, 62, 63, 64, 65, 68
Percy, Henry, Earl of Northumberland, 86
Peru, 59
Philip, King of Spain, 60, 106
Pierce, Jane 126
Plymouth, 86, 106, 124
Pollard, Sir Lewis, 75
Pope, 44
Port Royal, 18, 22
Portuguese ambassador, 78
Powell, Winifred, 126
Powhatan, 136
Pratt, Roger, 128
Presbyterian, 40, 78
Prince Eric of Sweden, 116
Protestants, 2, 3, 4, 5, 7, 9, 10, 16, 17, 18, 19, 20, 21, 23, 29, 31, 32, 33, 37, 42, 43, 44, 45, 47, 48, 53, 55, 81, 85, 89, 92, 96
Puerto Rico, 129
Pyrenees, 25, 26, 27, 28, 34

R

Rabasteins garrison, 34
Raleigh, Adrian, 113
Raleigh, Bess Throckmorton, 111-123, 138; see below, Sir Walter Raleigh
Raleigh, Carew, 113, 123
Raleigh, Lord John, 113
Raleigh, Walter, the elder, 113;
wife, Catherine Champernown Gilbert, 113
Raleigh, Walter, Jr., 114
Raleigh, Sir Walter, Governor Jersey, 60, 67, 113, 114, 115, 116, 117, 118, 119, 120, 121, 122, 123, 128; see above, wife, Bess Raleigh
Rawley, Indian, 133
Rene de Laudonniere, 75
Ribault, John (Jean), 22, 75
Rich Mond, King's Party, 39
Richmond Palace, on Thames, 1
Riccio, David, 46, 48, 49, 51

Rich, Lady, 90
Rio de Janerio, 74
Roanoke Island, 131, 133, 134
Robart, clergyman, 75
Robsart, Amy, 61
Robsart, John, 61
Rowse, Anthony, 106, 107
Russell, Sir Francis, Earl of Bedford, 16, 30, 59, 82, 87, 88; wife, Margaret St. John
Russia, 5, 78

S

St. Andrews Church, Plymouth, 126
St. Augustine, Florida, 32
St. Bartholomew's Day, 80
St. Bride's Church, London, 128
St. Giles' Church, 46
St. John-de-Luz, 16, 70
St. John's River, Florida, 32, 130
St. Leger, John, 97; wife, Catherine Neville
St. Leger, Ursula, 100
St. Leger, Warham, 75, 99, 100
St. Mary's Church, Bideford, 97, 107, 108
St. Margaret's Church, Devon, 98
St. Peter's Chapel, 11
St. Pierre's Church, 18, 22
St. Simons Island, 130
St. Thomas Island, 85
Sackville, Earl of Dorset, 93
Salterne, John, mayor, 107
Salterne, William, 101
San Juan, Puerto Rico, 91
Sandys, Sir Edwin, 11
Sapello island, 130
Scottish Parliament, 41
Seymore, Queen Jane, 4
Sheffield, Douglas, 80
Sheen Palace, 61
Sherborne Castle, 118, 119, 120, 121, 122
Sidney, Sir Henry, Lord Lieutenant of Ireland, Lord President of Council of Wales, 42, 56-58, 72, 75; wife, see below
Sidney, Mary Dudley, Countess of Pembroke, 7, 57-68, 138
Sidney, Sir Philip, Governor of Flushing, Ireland, 64, 65, 66, 67, 68, 101
Skybeck Manor, Kent, 58
Skipton Castle, 86
Society of Merchants, 84
Spanish Armada, 88
Spicer, Edward, 126
Stafford, Baron and wife Ursula, 14

Index 177

Stafford, Dorothée, Seigneuress de Rocheford, 13-24, 138; see Sir William Stafford
Stafford, Sir Edward, 16, 23, 126
Stafford, Sir William, 13, 15, 16, 17, 21
Sterling Castle, 45, 47, 49, 51, 53
Stevenson, Cornelius, 80
Stewart, Esmé, Seigneur d'Abigny, Duke of Lennox, 53
Stewart, Henry, Lord Darnley, 37, 43, 45, 49
Stewart, Ludowick, Duke of Lennox, 54
Strait of Magellan, 85, 102, 104
Stuart, Mary, Queen of England, 20, 22
Stuart Ar(a)bella, 53, 92, 121
Stuckley, Jane, 75
Stuckley, John, 106

T

Tattersall College, 61
Tappan, Audrey, 126
Tavistock Manor, 84
Throckmorton, Sir Nicholas, 51, 72, 73, 111; wife, see above Anne Carew
Tower of London, 1, 7, 8, 58, 59, 73, 117, 121, 122, 137
Travers, Walter, 20
Trinidad, 119
Turner, artist, 107
Tyndall's Bible, 84

U

Underhill, Edward, 111
Utopia, 67

V

Valetta, Malta, 33
Viccars, Elizabeth, 126
Vintners' Company, 85
Villegaman, 30

W

Walsingham, Sir Francis, 23
Warren, Joan, 126
Warwick, Aunt, 91, 92
Werowance, 134
West, Thomas, 74
West Indies, 127
West Indies Company, 91
Westminster, 52, 90, 91, 93
Westmoreland, 94
Wharton, Lord, 86
White, John, Governor, 125, 126, 127, 128, 129, 132, 133

Whitehall Palace, 4
Whittingham, William, chaplain, 76
William the Conqueror, 70
Windsor Castle, 92
Winter, George, 59
Winter, William, 59, 72, 74
Woman's Abbey, Caen, 70
Wood, Agnes, 126
Woodcarne, 64, 99

Z

Zucchero, artist, 112
Zurich, 83

MELLEN LIVES

1. Aaron Milavec, **A Pilgrim Experiences the World's Religions: Discovering the Human Faces of the Hidden God**
2. Jean Koberlin, **A Spiritual Encounter With The Holy One**
3. Daniel Evans Taylor, **The Autobiography of Daniel Evans Taylor**
4. Mildred Bennett, **The Autobiography of Mildred Bennett, The Early Years: The Winter is Past**
5. Ishvani Hamilton, **My Early Life**
6. John M. Naish, **A Physician's Eye**
7. Cyril Hart, **An Autobiography and Personal Philosophy of a Retired Physician**
8. Jane Lester, **An American College Girl in Hitler's Germany: A Memoir**
9. Jack Wilson, **Diary of an Army Baker, Quartermaster Corps, Southwest Pacific, 1942-1945**, John Howard Wilson, Jr. (ed.)
10. Jo A. Baldwin, **Seven Signature Sermons by a Tuning Woman Preacher of the Gospel**
11. Elizabeth Darracott Wheeler, **Ten Remarkable Women of the Tudor Courts and Their Influence in Founding the New World, 1530-1630**

3